The Railway Murders

The Railway Murders

Significant Cases in British Railway History

Malcolm Clegg

PEN & SWORD TRANSPORT

AN IMPRINT OF PEN & SWORD BOOKS LTD.
YORKSHIRE – PHILADELPHIA

First published in Great Britain in 2026 by
Pen & Sword Transport
An imprint of Pen & Sword Books Limited
Yorkshire – Philadelphia

ISBN 978 1 03619 222 8

A CIP catalogue record for this book is
available from the British Library.

Typeset by Mac Style
Printed and bound in India by Replika Press Pvt. Ltd.

The Publisher's authorised representative in the EU for product
safety is Authorised Rep Compliance Ltd., Ground Floor,
71 Lower Baggot Street, Dublin D02 P593, Ireland.
www.arccompliance.com

For a complete list of Pen & Sword titles please contact:

PEN & SWORD BOOKS LIMITED
47 Church Street, Barnsley, South Yorkshire, S70 2AS, England
E-mail: enquiries@pen-and-sword.co.uk
Website: www.pen-and-sword.co.uk
or
PEN AND SWORD BOOKS
1950 Lawrence Road, Havertown, PA 19083, USA
E-mail: uspen-and-sword@casematepublishers.com
Website: www.penandswordbooks.com

Contents

Preface

Without a doubt, one of the most serious crimes which can occur in society as a whole is the unlawful killing of a human being by another, usually referred to as murder or homicide. Sadly, such crimes are all too common and can be committed at anytime, anywhere, including on the railway networks.

This book examines well over 100 murders and attempted murders committed either upon the railways of England, Scotland and Wales, or closely associated with and involving the railways in one way or another. In some instances, persons charged with wilful murder have been acquitted but found to be guilty of a lesser charge, such as manslaughter. Such examples are also included in this book.

Over the years, numerous railway employees have been blamed for fatal 'railway accidents' which have resulted in criminal convictions for manslaughter. The staff members most likely to be deemed culpable in such cases by the nature of their job, are train-drivers, signalmen, and track maintenance workers. Accidents of this nature invariably involve negligence, carelessness or the breach of rules and regulations by members of staff. Such cases are not direct physical attacks on individuals with intent to harm them, consequently they are not included in this book.

The vast majority of the information contained in this book has been obtained through many months of painstaking research, carried out by delving into old newspaper archives. In addition, I have used information from the archives of the British Transport Police History Group (btphg. org.uk) and internet websites such as The National Archives. All the cases are true and are now a part of our nation's history, and the history of the railways.

Introduction

Development of the Railways

Most of the railways in Britain were built during the nineteenth century by private railway companies. Many of the small railway companies were quickly absorbed into larger companies before being merged to form even bigger companies, which eventually led to a comprehensive nationwide railway network.

By the beginning of the twentieth century, well over 100 different railway companies were operating in Britain on over 22,000 miles of track. Although all these companies were privately owned, their construction had been approved and authorised by parliament, and their safety, together with the way they operated, was strictly monitored, controlled and regulated by government legislation.

In 1912, Britain began making preparations for the possibility of a military conflict, due to civil unrest in Europe. It was realised that in the event of war being declared, the railways would play a vital role in mobilising the British army. The large-scale movement of over 600,000 men, together with vast amounts of equipment and munitions would have to be embarked upon almost immediately, and it was felt that the logistical challenges to mobilise such an army could not be successfully achieved by over 100 different railway companies acting independently.

After much discussion, it was decided that should a military conflict in Europe materialise, it would be necessary for the whole railway network to be taken under government control. This led to the formation of a new body, the Railway Executive Committee (REC) of the government, which would control the railways in the event of war.

Sadly, the predicted military conflict in Europe did emerge and 28 June 1914 saw the outbreak of the First World War. Britain was drawn into the conflict and declared war on Germany on 4 August 1914. Immediately, the REC took over the operation of Britain's entire railway network, placing it under government control. The government decided that during the war, the day to day running of the railways would best be met by the British army and in 1915 the Railway Operating Division (ROD) of the British army was created.

In essence, the ROD was a new division of the Royal Engineers. Its sole purpose was to control and operate the railways in the various theatres of war both at home and abroad and it operated very successfully for the duration of the conflict.

Although November 1918 saw the end of the war, Britain's railway network was in no fit state to be handed back to the private companies due to being run down by lack of maintenance, over use, and war damage inflicted during the conflict. Suggestions were put forward for a plan to nationalise the railways, but after careful consideration, the idea was rejected, and the railway network temporarily remained under the control of the REC, pending a solution.

1921 saw the introduction of The Railways Act which authorised the amalgamation of more than 120 railway companies which had been operating in Britain before the war into just four large privately owned companies. This, it was said, would make the railway network easier to manage and prevent unnecessary rivalry between the former companies. It was an alternative to nationalising the railways completely. The 1921 Railways Act, which became known as the Railway Groupings Act came into effect on 1 January 1923 and the four new private railway companies which became known as the 'Big Four' emerged.

The companies concerned, in order of size and starting with the largest, were the London, Midland and Scottish Railway (LMS), the London and North-Eastern Railway (LNER), the Great Western Railway (GWR) and the Southern Railway (SR).

Most railway companies incorporated into the big four had previously employed a considerable number of railway policemen and in January 1923 these officers, which exceeded 3,000 in total, were absorbed into four new Railway Police Forces, created specifically to police each of the big four railway companies.

The big four railway companies continued to operate Britain's railway network until September 1939, when the outbreak of the Second World

War once again dictated that the operation of the railways should come under government control. Consequently, another REC was set up to administer the railways for the duration of the conflict.

At the end of the war, Britain's railways were in an appalling state due to severe war damage, neglect and lack of maintenance throughout the six-year conflict. As a result, the government decided that there was little alternative other than to fully nationalise the whole railway network and rebuild it with state funding. This course of action was adopted, the railways were nationalised and started operating under its new name, British Railways (BR), as and from 1 January 1948.

A new police force, the British Transport Commission Police (BTCP) was created to police the whole railway network, together with other nationalised transport institutions. Officers who had previously served in the big four railway police forces became an integral part of this new police force which became operational in January 1949. Police officers who had previously served at docks, ports, harbours and on the canal network in Britain, were also absorbed into the new force. In 1963, the BTCP was renamed the British Transport Police (BTP) and it has continued policing the railways to the present day.

The name 'British Railways' was shortened to 'British Rail' in 1965, and the state-owned enterprise continued to operate the railways until it was privatised in stages by the government between 1994 and 1997.

Network Rail, which currently owns and manages twenty of the largest railway stations in the country, as well as being responsible for the entire railway track, associated structures, and signalling, was not privatised in the 1990s, and continues to operate as a government owned company. The trains which run on Britain's railways today are not owned by Network Rail or by the private operating companies, but instead are owned and leased by private rolling stock leasing companies.

The year 2024 saw Britain's Conservative government replaced by a new Labour government which quickly announced that consideration was being given to re-nationalise Britain's Railways entirely. It seems likely therefore, that further changes to the ownership of the railway network will be on the horizon.

Capital Punishment

At the beginning of nineteenth century, the 'Bloody Code' was a series of laws in England, Wales and Ireland whereby the death penalty was mandatory for a wide range of crimes. The laws were relaxed in 1823 when the death penalty became discretionary for all crimes except treason and murder. Further reforms were carried out during the 1820s by Sir Robert Peel, the Home Secretary, and by 1841 only murder and treason remained capital crimes punishable by the death penalty.

Public executions were carried out during the nineteenth century and members of the public were encouraged to gather and witness deaths by hanging as it was deemed to act as a deterrent to people contemplating the crime of murder. Huge crowds of people flocked to witness public executions which was considered a form of public entertainment and an educational event. The events even attracted market stalls, alcohol consumption and souvenir sales. By the 1850s, public executions had diminished considerably, although ninety-five public executions were still carried out during the decade. Public executions were abolished during the 1860s, and the last public hanging on mainland Britain took place in 1868.

Capital punishment (death by hanging) continued to be a mandatory sentence for anyone convicted of murder until it was suspended in Britain in 1965 before being finally abolished in 1969 (1973 in Northern Ireland). Since abolition of the death penalty, the mandatory sentence for the offence of murder has been life imprisonment.

The cases referred to in this book give an insight into a variety of different murders and attempted murders which have been committed on the railway, both solved and unsolved. It should be remembered that in the nineteenth and early twentieth century, murders and other serious crimes were extremely difficult to solve, unless there were eye witnesses to the events, or those responsible admitted their guilt. Forensic science was in its infancy, fingerprint evidence, and blood grouping had not been developed and DNA evidence to solve murder cases was not available until the 1980s.

Having said that, some of the early murder cases were solved, and the culprits suffered the harsh consequences of their actions. Sadly, other such crimes remain undetected to this day. Although the topic of this book is rather gruesome, the circumstances surrounding the crimes are quite captivating and many of the cases referred to are somewhat compelling and intriguing.

Chapter 1

Early Railway Murders

The First Railway Murder

The first railway murder to have been committed anywhere in the world is believed to have taken place on the outskirts of Glasgow in 1840. The circumstances leading up to and surrounding the event are as follows.

In July 1838, an Act of Parliament was passed, which authorised the building of a 46 mile (74km) long railway from Edinburgh (Haymarket) to Glasgow, the Edinburgh and Glasgow Railway. Construction started almost immediately and continued until the railway was completed. It was officially opened on 21 February 1842.

Almost all railway construction in the 1840s was carried out manually by vast numbers of 'navvies', some of whom were descendants of the former navigators (where the name navvies is derived from), who had built Britain's canal networks a few years earlier. They were joined by local labourers as well as itinerant labourers who travelled all over the country, seeking work wherever new railways were being built. There were vast numbers of immigrants from Ireland who fled the poverty of their homeland, to seek decent wages working as railway navvies. Although most navvies were hard workers, they were a rough bunch, usually heavy drinkers who were frequently drunk and often violent. As they worked their way around the country, they were generally feared by the public at large and often wrought havoc in their wake. Having said that, they were forced to live in appalling conditions such as over-crowded huts, shelters, tents and shacks alongside the railways on which they were working. It was commonplace to see English, Scottish and Irish navvies fighting and brawling amongst themselves and with each other. Some navvies were even accompanied by their wives and families as they worked their way from one construction site to another. Nevertheless, despite their behaviour, without the navvies, the railways in Britain would never have been built.

Navvies were not employed directly by the railway companies for whom they were working but were engaged by private contractors on behalf of the companies. These private contractors also employed site superintendents to oversee the work being carried out by the navvies as well as being responsible for their conduct and discipline. Any breaches of discipline or sub-standard workmanship was usually punished by instant dismissal. Most site superintendents were themselves tough men, very experienced and hard taskmasters. They usually worked all over the country where new railways were being built. Their reputation often preceded them as they moved from one railway to another over the years. The navvies themselves usually carried out their daily work in gangs, primarily consisting of twelve men, known as butty gangs. There was no official gang foreman, and all the men were deemed to be of equal status. They did however jointly elect one member of the gang as an unofficial leader and spokesperson. He had the task of keeping the gang in check and collecting wages from the site superintendent to distribute equally amongst the men. The men were left to their own devices to sort out shirkers and lazy workers which was usually done by fisticuffs.

In December 1840, a site Superintendent by the name of John Green started work on the Edinburgh to Glasgow railway which was in the final stages of construction. Mr Green had worked on several railways in England during their construction and he had a reputation of being a strict boss and hard taskmaster whilst in charge of the navvies.

He started working for the Edinburgh and Glasgow Railway Company on 9 December 1840 at Crosshill, near Bishopsbridge, approximately three miles outside Glasgow. He was placed in charge of several butty gangs, the large majority of whom were Irish. On his very first day, he started to experience intimidation from a few of the workers and was subject to stones and other objects being thrown at him. This behaviour was not uncommon when taking charge of a new site. The following morning, John Green arrived on site shortly before seven o'clock. It was a cold damp winter's day, still dark but daylight was just starting to break. As he approached the site, he saw several navvies standing in a group. As he approached, most of them dispersed as if going to start work but a few stayed behind, talking to each other.

As he approached the group of men. he was heard to say; 'What do you think of the weather, my lads? – it's going to be wet'. One of the men replied, 'Yes it's going to be a wet morning'. Green continued walking past the men, and when his back was to them, one of the men struck him violently over the head with an iron bar. His hat fell off and he slumped to the ground. Another one of the men then started stamping on his body before repeatedly putting the boot in. The man with the iron bar continued to strike Green viciously about the head and body. After giving Green a horrific beating, both men fled the scene and ran away. John Green died less than one hour later, having been battered to death. The incident was witnessed by several people, including Frank Rooney, a Works Supervisor and another Site Superintendent.

The local Scottish Sheriff (a member of the judiciary) later visited the site, along with a company of soldiers from the 58th Foot Regiment, and a total of twenty-three Irish labourers were arrested and taken into custody. The two men who had fled the scene were later named as Dennis Doolan, aged 29 a native of King's County, Ireland, and Patrick Redding, aged 25, a native of Tipperary. Their details were circulated as wanted for questioning in relation to the murder of John Green.

Several days later, Patrick Redding was arrested in England and escorted back to Glasgow. In January 1841, over three weeks after murder, Dennis Doolan was arrested in Liverpool whilst trying to make his way to America. When Doolan was initially arrested, he denied being Dennis Doolan and he gave his name as Dennis Hyde. The police did not believe him, so he was escorted from Liverpool to Glasgow by steamship, accompanied by two police officers from Liverpool. During the journey he maintained that his name was Hyde, that nobody in Glasgow would identify him as Doolan, and that they, the police would have to pay his fare back to Liverpool. Doolan was however positively identified upon his arrival in Glasgow and remanded in custody at Glasgow Prison.

A case against Doolan and Redding was quickly established in which it was concluded that the murder had been premeditated to enable the navvies to rid themselves of the new superintendent who had been put in charge of them, and who, by his reputation, they considered would be difficult to work for and a hard taskmaster. Both men were later charged with the wilful murder of John Green.

A third man arrested immediately after the murder took place was James Hickie from County Carlow, Ireland. He was also charged with the wilful murder of Green after it was established that he had obtained an iron bar from a smithy at the railway site and handed it to Redding for use as the murder weapon. Three other men, John Campbell, Patrick Cosgrove and George Cox were also charged in connection with the murder.

Cosgrove and Cox were also referred to as Kinnary and Cook in some newspapers printed at the time. Other defendants may also have been referred to by different names. The reason for these inconsistencies is because Irish navvies frequently used an alias when travelling from place to place.

All of the men stated their intention to plead 'Not Guilty' to wilful murder, and first rate legal representation was paid for by the Irish labourers working on the Edinburgh to Glasgow railway, who each contributed 3d a week (approximately £2 a week today) from the date of the alleged murder until the date of the court hearing, to secure the services of Patrick Robertson and J.H. Maxwell who were considered to be two of the top advocates in Glasgow, to represent the accused.

The murder trial took place at the Circuit Court in Glasgow on Monday 22 March 1841. Three of the defendants, Campbell, Cosgrove and Cox turned Queen's Evidence and gave evidence at the trial, taking care not to implicate themselves. The other three defendants pleaded 'Not Guilty' to the charge of wilful murder, despite overwhelming mass of evidence being produced by the prosecution. Consequently, no evidence was offered by the defence who accepted the principal facts but each of the defendants laid the guilt and blame for the murder on each other.

After a hearing which had lasted for twelve hours it took the jury just forty-five minutes, to find Dennis Doolan, Patrick Redding (both unanimous verdicts) and James Hickie (majority verdict) guilty of the wilful murder of John Green. A unanimous recommendation of mercy was made in respect of the defendant Hickie. All three men were sentenced to death by hanging and the judge directed that the sentence was to be carried out alongside the railway line at Crosshill where the murder had taken place.

The three men were transported to Glasgow Prison to await execution. The death sentence imposed on Hickie was later commuted to transportation to a penal colony for life. The execution of Doolan and Redding was set to take place on Friday14 May 1841.

On Thursday 13 May 1841, scaffolding from Glasgow Prison was transported to the execution site where the gallows were erected. Soldiers remained at the site until the following day as a security precaution.

That evening at Glasgow Prison, Bishop Murdock (a Roman Catholic Bishop), remained with Doolan and Redding until ten o'clock. After Bishop Murdock left, three laymen remained with the prisoners all night. The prisoners went to bed at one o'clock in the morning and rested until four o'clock but neither of them slept. They rose and resumed their devotions until it was time for them to prepare for their departure. At eight minutes before eight o'clock, having previously been handcuffed and manacled together with strong chain by the legs, they were brought out of the cell accompanied by Bishop Murdock and another Roman Catholic priest. Both men were escorted through the judiciary court hall and out of the front of the building.

At eight o'clock precisely, a procession left Glasgow Prison bound for Crosshill. The composition of the procession was as follows; from the front – Cavalry, City Marshal, a large open carriage in which the two accused were loosely pinioned in an elevated position so they could be easily seen by spectators as the procession passed by. The open carriage also carried their religious instructors. The carriage was followed by more cavalry, the executioner, the Sheriff, Lord Provost, magistrates and more cavalry. Along the entire length of the procession, both the right and left sides were flanked by cavalry (inside), infantry (centre) and police (outside). The procession proceeded up the Saltmarket, the High Street and along Kirkintilloch Road to Bishopsbridge, where a guard of infantry with Mr Sheriff Bell were already present. The total number of military escorts was estimated at being between 600 and 700 infantry and 200 cavalry. Two troops of soldiers from the 4th Dragoon Guards were also present. The procession reached its destination at a quarter to ten.

After some time spent in religious devotion with Bishop Murdock, both men confessed to the murder of John Green and begged his forgiveness.

They both insisted that they had never intended to murder Green when they originally planned the attack, but they did intend to give him a sound beating which went too far.

The executioner proceeded to do his duty. He gave Redding, who was a small slender man, about 18 inches more of a drop than he did Doolan, who was stout and heavy. After the clergymen left the condemned men, the executioner placed the ropes around their necks. Doolan then turned to Redding to bid him farewell, and as he did so, the knot on the noose of the rope slipped from under his left ear to the back of his neck just as the execution took place. The consequence was that he struggled severely, enduring great suffering for some time dangling and kicking on the end of the rope before he eventually died of strangulation. Redding on the other hand died almost instantly after a clean drop. The execution took place at five minutes before ten o'clock, and the bodies were left hanging for some forty-five minutes before being taken down. Both bodies were placed in coffins and transported to Glasgow Prison where they were interred within the precincts of the prison that same evening. The executioner was later asked why he had almost botched the hanging of Doolan, and he placed the blame entirely on the fact that the rope was too hard. A large crowd turned out to watch the public execution. The actual numbers may have been in excess of 100,000. Newspaper reports and estimates given at the time varied enormously and spectator numbers were put between 50,000 and 150,000. In any event, the mass of the population present was greater than had ever been seen within the city or in the vicinity of Glasgow. Everything passed over without the slightest incident, and there was not the slightest sign of any riots, which had been feared by some.

Gruesome Parcels Sent by Train

In 1842, Joseph Timperley was living with his wife and family at the Altrincham Union Workhouse at Knutsford in Cheshire. The workhouse was home to over 300 inmates.

On 15 April that year, a brown paper parcel was delivered by a horse drawn railway vehicle to the workhouse, addressed to Joseph Timperley. The parcel had been sent by train from Euston Railway Station in London.

After removing the outer wrapping paper from the parcel, Joseph discovered a wooden box. Upon opening the box, to his horror and disbelief, he found the dead body of a baby boy, wrapped in a shawl and some fine linen, which was covered in dry blood. Also inside the box was a hand-written note on a piece of paper which said, 'You will do your wife a favour by burying this'. The matter was immediately reported to the local police.

A police investigation resulted in officers visiting the home of a Mr Catley, a wealthy gentleman who lived in a large house in Leytonstone, East London. There, they interviewed Sarah Drake, aged 27, who also lived there. She was employed by Mr Catley as a cook and housekeeper, the most senior servant in the household.

Seeing the police officers, Sarah became very distressed, and when interviewed, she admitted sending the parcel to Joseph Timperley. She was subsequently arrested and taken to a local police station. Whilst in custody, she informed police that the previous year, whilst working for Mr Catley, she met Joseph Timperley, who was working in London. They had a relationship which resulted in Sarah becoming pregnant. Timperley then told Sarah that he was already married, and he had decided to move back to Cheshire to live with his wife and family.

Sarah did not tell anyone in the house where she worked about her pregnancy, and nobody made any mention of it until it became too obvious to ignore. Servants in the house then started to gossip about her being in the family way but she ignored them. In April 1842, she gave birth to a baby boy, whilst alone and in her room. She told police that the baby was dead when it was born, and she did not know what to do with it. It was then that she decided to send it to Joseph Timperley to dispose of it, because he was the child's father.

Sarah told police that she later approached a fellow servant and asked him if he could get her a wooden box and some brown wrapping paper as she wanted to send some personal items to a relative living in the country. The servant obtained the pine box and gave it to Sarah along with the wrapping paper.

Sarah admitted wrapping the dead baby in a shawl and some linen, before placing it in the box, together with the note which she had written to Joseph Timperley. She then wrapped the box in the wrapping paper.

A short time later, she handed the parcel to another servant who was employed as a footman. She asked him to write the name and address of Mr Timperley on the outside of the parcel, which he did. The footman later took the parcel, on behalf of Sarah, to Euston Station parcels office to be sent to its destination in Cheshire. Both the servant who supplied the box and wrapping paper to Sarah, and the footman who took it to Euston Station were later interviewed by police and they confirmed that what Sarah had told them was correct.

A postmortem on the child's body was carried out by Watson Baird, a surgeon who lived in Knutsford. He expressed his belief that the infant was in fact born alive. He went on to say that in his opinion, it was a fully developed, healthy male child. There were marks of compression on the neck of the baby. On the right side was the mark of a thumb, and on the left side, marks of fingers. He expressed his opinion that the death was 'occasioned by this violent compression', and that the injuries were caused whilst the child was alive. Detectives presented these findings to Sara Drake, but she strongly denied killing her baby, insisting that the baby was dead when it was born.

In view of the findings of Mr Watson Baird during the postmortem, and despite denials by Sarah Drake about killing her baby, she remained in custody until she appeared before Ilford magistrates court in Essex, charged with wilful murder. The whole facts of the case were produced in evidence and at the conclusion of the hearing, the prisoner was asked if she wished to say anything in answer to the charge, the magistrate at the same time cautioning her that what she said would be taken down and produced in evidence against her at her trial. The prisoner in a faint tone of voice replied that she had nothing to say. The magistrate said that it was his painful duty to commit her to stand trial upon a charge of wilful murder.

The accused appeared before the Central Criminal Court (Old Bailey) London on the 17 May 1842. The charge of wilful murder was not proceeded with, but she was found guilty of concealing the birth of her dead male child and sentenced to six months imprisonment with hard labour.

Just over two years later, in December 1844, Sarah Drake's sister Mary Burton received a box which had been delivered to her home. Upon opening the box, she also experienced a horrific discovery when she found the dead body of a newly born male child inside. Sarah was again questioned at great length by police about this second almost identical discovery of another dead baby boy, sent this time to her sister, and although she was very strongly suspected of being responsible for this appalling act, no action was ever taken against her due to lack of evidence.

Five years later, however, in December 1849, Sarah Drake was again back in the dock when she appeared before the Central Criminal Court in London charged with the wilful murder of yet another illegitimate child, her son Louis Drake aged 2. Once again, the cause of death was due to strangulation. Sarah was represented by an eminent barrister, Mr Collier. A plea of 'not guilty on the grounds of insanity' was entered on her behalf, and despite no witnesses being called to give evidence for the defence, she was found not guilty of wilful murder, on the grounds of temporary insanity. She was confined to the notorious Bedlam Lunatic Asylum, during Her Majesty's Pleasure.

Sarah Drake was not, as expected, incarcerated for the rest of her life. After serving less than ten years in the asylum, she was released and continued living in London until her death in 1891 at the age of 77. Many people at the time, and subsequently, believe that Sarah Drake was extremely lucky to have escaped the hangman's noose.

In December 1843, not long after the first incident involving Sarah Drake, another parcel was sent by train from London to Winchester on the South Western Railway. The parcel was addressed to a Mr Muspratt, the proprietor of a hardware shop in the city. When an attempt was made to deliver the parcel, it transpired that the shop was no longer owned by Mr Muspratt, who had recently died, so the parcel was returned to Winchester Station parcels office as 'undelivered'.

On the 5 January 1844, A South Western Railway Police Constable inspected the parcel with a view to establishing details of the person who sent it. Upon opening the parcel, the constable found it to contain a wicker basket. Inside the basket was a quantity of loose paper. Beneath the paper, he found a white calico bag, tied at the neck with a piece of white tape. The bag was strongly scented with musk. Inside this bag, the constable found another bag made of white oilskin. This bag was also tied at the neck, but with a piece of red tape. Upon opening the oilskin bag and to his horror, he discovered what appeared to be the body of a newly-born male child. It was not decomposed and presented no visible marks of external violence. Superintendent J.B. Dalby of the South Western Railway Police attended the scene and immediately started a murder investigation.

An inquest was held later that afternoon before the Winchester Coroner Mr J.W. Todd, who adjourned the enquiry pending further enquiries by Superintendent Dalby. On Monday 22 January, the adjourned enquiry was proceeded with at the White Swan public house.

Mr Smith, a surgeon, stated that he had made a postmortem examination of the body. He stated that the lungs floated in water, which clearly proved that the child was born alive. There were some slight abrasions on the arms, which the surgeon believed had been caused whilst packing up the child whilst still alive. The head was the most decomposed part of the body, which led him to believe that injuries to the head may have been inflicted wilfully, although considering all the circumstances, he could not say for certain whether violence had been used, or whether the infant had died due to neglect, presumably by the parent.

Superintendent Dalby stated that he had made the most diligent enquiries and established that the basket in which the child was sent had been bought from a shop at 168 Oxford Street in London, but Mr Cuttings, the shop owner, had no idea as to who bought the basket or when it was sold. Superintendent Dalby went on to say that subsequent enquiries and efforts made by him were to no avail.

The coroner observed that it was pointless to carry the inquiry any further. The railway company had done their best to discover the guilty party, but to no avail. It was very probable, from the precautions which had been taken by the party who forwarded the parcel, they would never be discovered and therefore details surrounding the death of the child could not be established. The jury then returned an open verdict, that the deceased child had been sent down from London by the South Western Railway to Winchester, but by whom so sent, or by what means it came to its death, there was no evidence to show. The case remained unsolved.

Less than three years later, a similar incident occurred whereby another package containing the body of a child was sent by train.

On Friday 20 November 1846, a parcel was taken to Nottingham Railway Station by an unknown young woman with short hair and a dark complexion who handed it to Mr Willoughby, a railway porter who was on duty in the station parcels office. The parcel was addressed to a Mr W.J. Smith at an address in Suffolk.

The young lady specifically told Willoughby that the parcel was very fragile, and it should not be placed amongst other parcels or crushed. She stated it should be conveyed with great care, and if possible be put on a seat along with the passengers. The parcels office was very busy at the time, so porter Willoughby labelled the parcel as fragile and put it to one side. The parcel was later put on a London bound train, from where it would be forwarded on to its destination in Suffolk.

On Thursday 26 November, the parcel arrived back in Nottingham at 2.30 am on a night mail train. The parcel was endorsed 'Undelivered – Return to Sender'. Porter Willoughby, who just happened to be on duty again that night, remembered receiving the parcel from the young woman the previous week, so he unwrapped it to establish who has sent it. Inside the parcel he found a wicker basket. Upon closer inspection, to his shock and repulsion, Willoughby saw a dead infant inside the basket. The mouth appeared to have had considerable moisture in it, and parts of the face had become green and mouldy. Willoughby was horrified and nauseated by what he had found.

Beneath the infant was a quantity of cloths and straw, together with a letter addressed to 'W.J. Smith, Esq; Suffolk.' The letter, which was written in a decent handwriting, requested that the father of the infant should take care of it, and it warned him against seducing anyone as he had done her. The basket with the child and letter was later handed over to the police who were quickly in attendance. A Coroner's Court was assembled but adjourned until the following Saturday to allow a postmortem examination to take place.

This was later carried out by Mr W. Yates, a surgeon at the Nottingham Dispensary, who concluded that the infant was a fine and well-formed female about a week old. There were no marks of violence upon the body. It was his opinion that the body had been put into the basket alive, and had died partially through want of nourishment, partially owing to cold, and partially from the effects of an overdose of opiate.

The inquest was held, after which it was adjourned sine-die (an undetermined length of time) by the coroner to allow further enquiries to be made by Superintendent Rogerson of the Nottingham Police. Despite extensive enquiries and a full investigation, charges were never brought against any individual in connection with this matter and the case remained unsolved.

Killer Thwarted by Railway Telegraph

The world's first electric telegraph system was invented by Sir William Fothergill Cook and Charles Wheatstone during the 1830s and installed on the GWR to enable signal boxes along the track to communicate with each other to monitor and control the movement of trains. The first section of this new telegraph system was installed from Paddington to West Drayton, some 20 miles (32km), and was completed in 1843, using overhead cables supported by telegraph poles. It proved to be a complete success and by 1850 similar telegraph systems had been introduced on more than half of Britain's railway network.

The public became aware of the true value of this new communications device a year after it had been installed, when on 6 August 1844 a message was sent by the GWR telegraph system that Queen Victoria had given birth at Windsor Castle to her second son, Alfred, who would later become the Duke of Edinburgh. The message was quickly received in London to the jubilation of anxious ministers and members of the public.

Although primarily designed for the day-to-day running of the railways, it was soon realised that the electric telegraph system had a wide range of other benefits, which included detecting crime by affording assistance to police officers in their pursuit of dangerous criminals, particularly over long distances. In an ironic twist of fate, the GWR telegraph system itself was used for precisely that purpose, to solve a serious local crime committed in Slough, less than six months after it had been installed. The crime in question was a murder, which entered the history books as being the first ever crime to be solved as a direct result of using the electric telegraph.

On New Year's Day 1845, a married man, John Tawell, murdered his mistress Sarah Hart by poisoning her, after administering a quantity of prussic acid (hydrogen cyanide) which was contained in a medicinal compound called Scheels acid, used in the treatment of varicose veins.

Tawell had visited the home of Miss Hart in Salt Hill near Slough and laced a glass of stout with the cyanide which she drank as they toasted the New Year. As the poison began to take effect, Tawell left the cottage and made his way to Slough Railway Station to catch a train home to London, leaving Miss Hart alone to suffer an agonising death. After he had left the cottage, Miss Hart somehow managed to raise the alarm by contacting the Reverend E.T. Champness, her neighbour and a local vicar. She gave a description of Tawell to the reverend on her deathbed and as a result, he immediately made his way to Slough Railway Station. He arrived at Slough Station just in time to see a man who he assumed to be Tawell, boarding the 7.42pm train to London Paddington.

Without further ado, the reverend immediately summoned Mr Howell, the Station Master who acted astutely and arranged for what was to become an historic message to be sent to Paddington. The message read:

A murder has just been committed at Salt Hill and the suspected murderer was seen to take a first-class ticket for London by train which left Slough at 7.42pm for London. He is in the garb [clothing] of a Quaker with a brown greatcoat on which reaches down to his feet. He is in the last compartment of the second first-class carriage'.

A short time later, the telegraph clerk at Slough received a reply to the telegram which read as follows: 'The up train has arrived and a person answering in every respect the description given by telegraph came out of the compartment mentioned. The man got into a New Road omnibus and Sergeant Williams into the same'.

In the meantime, having received the original message at Paddington, the quick-thinking telegraph clerk handed the message to a telegraph messenger-boy who ran to Police Sergeant Bill Williams of the GWR Police and handed him the message. Williams placed a civilian coat over his uniform and met the train as it arrived from Slough. He saw a man matching the description he had been given alight from a first-class carriage and leave the station. Williams followed the man who boarded a horse-drawn bus outside the station. Williams followed the man onto the bus and sat behind him. After travelling across London, Tawell alighted from the bus on the corner of Princess Street before entering a lodging-house in Scott's Yard near Cannon Street. Williams followed discreetly, taking care not to arouse Tawell's suspicions.

After satisfying himself that the lodging house was Tawell's home, Williams returned to Paddington to confirm the authenticity of the telegram and ensure that a murder had in fact taken place. After confirming these facts, Williams liaised with Inspector Wiggins of the Metropolitan Police at Paddington Green police station.

The following morning, Wiggins, in company with Williams, visited the lodging house in Scott's Yard but Tawell was not at home. Shortly afterwards, Williams spotted Tawell having breakfast in the nearby Jerusalem Coffee House. Wiggins went inside and escorted Tawell from the premises whilst Williams waited outside. Tawell denied being in Slough the previous day and denied knowing anyone who lived there. He denied all knowledge of the murder which had taken place. Williams identified Tawell as the person he had seen alighting from the train the previous day and who he followed to the address in Scott's Yard. As a result, Wiggins arrested Tawell.

John Tawell appeared before the Aylesbury Assize Court on 12 March 1845, where he pleaded not guilty to a charge of the wilful murder of Sarah Hart. He was subsequently found guilty and sentenced to death by hanging. On 28 March, the sentence was carried out at a public execution in Aylesbury before a crowd of over 2,000 spectators. Prior to the execution taking place, Tawell made a full written confession in the presence of a priest, which included the fact that he had made another unsuccessful attempt to murder Sarah Hart the previous September.

John Tawell had made history as being the first criminal ever to have been apprehended as a direct result of the electric telegraph.

Murder and Riot on the North British Railway

During the early years of railway construction, large numbers of Irish navvies were employed to carry out the hard manual labour, often working in extremely harsh conditions. Many newspapers at the time reported incidents involving drunkenness, violence, riotous behaviour and general disorder involving these navvies. Their behaviour was tolerated by a government who considered it to be a price worth paying to construct a railway network necessary to meet the requirements of the industrial revolution, but conflicts often took place between the Irish navvies and groups of non-Irish railway workers.

One such incident took place in 1846, just outside Fushiebridge, about eleven miles south of Edinburgh. This incident cumulated in the murder of Police Constable Richard Pace, a police officer in the Edinburgh Shire Constabulary which existed at that time, and serious injury being inflicted upon Police Constable John Veitch, a railway policeman who was with him.

At about midnight on Saturday, 7 March 1846, two navvies who were employed in the construction of a North British Railway branch line from Edinburgh to Hawick were arrested alongside the railway near Fushiebridge and taken into custody where they were charged with stealing watches belonging to non-Irish railway workers who were also involved in the construction of the railway. They were lodged in the cells at the County Police Station at Gorebridge. Word of their arrest quickly spread amongst the community of Irish navvies who lived in huts alongside the railway.

In the early hours of Sunday morning, approximately 300 navvies armed with pickaxes, clubs and other weapons stormed the police station, demanding the release of their work colleagues. On duty inside the police station and in charge of the prisoners were Sergeant Brown, a Railway Police Officer, and Constable Christie from the local County Constabulary. One of the navvies pointed a pistol to the head of Sergeant Brown and threatened to shoot him unless the prisoners were released. PC Christie was attacked and sustained extensive injuries resulting from of a severe beating handed out by some of the men. The officers still refused to unlock the cell, so the navvies broke open the cell door and released their comrades. The intruders and prisoners left the police station and marched in the direction of Fushiebridge some half a mile away, where they were met by police constables Richard Pace, the district patrol officer, and John Veitch, a railway constable.

The two officers immediately came under a savage attack from the navvies and were both subject to serious assaults. One of the men struck Constable Pace on the back of his head with a pickaxe handle which caused a severe fracture to the skull. His skull was in fact split wide open. Constable Veitch was kicked and severely beaten before managing to escape. Two passersby later found the two officers. PC Pace was carried to his home where he died shortly afterwards due to the injuries he had sustained during the attack. Although severely beaten, PC Veitch fortunately survived the attack.

Assistance was summoned and later that morning Sheriff Spiers and Sheriff Jamerson arrived at the scene, together with Superintendent List and officers of the Edinburgh-Shire County Police. Approximately twenty officers from the Edinburgh City Police also accompanied them. Sixty military dragoons were also sent to assist.

Nineteen Irish navvies were arrested by police with the assistance of the dragoons, and they were escorted to Edinburgh Prison.

About forty dragoons and a large constabulary force remained in the area for the remainder of the day, and throughout the Sunday night to guard against further disturbances, in part due to the many Scottish and English workers threatening to take action against the Irish navvies to avenge their countrymen.

At about eight o'clock on the Monday morning, the Scottish and English workers began to assemble in Edinburgh, determined to extact revenge on the Irish. Approximately 100 colliers from the Marquis of Lothian's coal mines joined them. They formed into a procession of over 1,000 in number, having armed themselves with a variety of weapons which included pick-shafts, spade handles, bludgeons and hammers.

To the sound of music from bagpipes and bugles, the men marched south from Edinburgh. As the procession approached Fushiebridge, the Irishmen, upon seeing them assembled in such numbers, took to their heels, fled across the country and escaped. Disappointed in not having a fight with the Irish, the Scots and English decided instead, to burn down the huts where they lived. At Crichton Moor, they burned six or eight, before proceeding to Borthwick Castle where they burned a similar number, in two different places.

Between thirty and forty of the County and City police officers were present, but owing to the overwhelming numbers of railway labourers, they did not interfere as the men continued to burn down the Irish huts. The wives of the Irish navvies were not attacked by the mob and remained in their huts as long as they could do so with safety, before gathering up their few personal belongings, household utensils and leaving. They then sat down dejected beside the smoking ruins of their homes. The Scots and English workers, having completed their work of destruction, returned quietly and by different routes to their homes. During that evening, nineteen arrests were made by both police and dragoons, of persons they suspected of being involved in the burning of the huts. The prisoners were taken to Edinburgh Prison, arriving about ten o'clock in the evening. About forty of the dragoons and a large constabulary force again remained at Fushiebridge during Monday night, to guard against further outrage. Many Irish navvies who had fled the rioting Scots and English workers earlier, went into Edinburgh that evening, where they congregated in the Cowgate public house to discuss 'paying the Scots back with interest'.

Between eight and nine o'clock the following morning, the Irish navvies began to pour from the Cowgate pub into the nearby streets. They were armed with heavy sticks and presented a rather formidable appearance as they proceeded along the public road towards Dalkeith.

Having been advised of their movements in advance, the Sheriff and the police met them several miles from Edinburgh. The Sheriff remonstrated with the men as to the impropriety of their conduct and advised them to return to Edinburgh. After speaking to them at some length, they eventually acceded to his advice and were escorted part of the way back to Edinburgh by Superintendent List and the officers under his command. Arrangements were made for the labourers to have a consultation with their contractors, to try to reach some sort of agreement to prevent any recurrence or further disturbances and conflicts taking place.

A further nine arrests were made that day, making a total number of twenty-eight in custody for being involved in burning the Irish huts. Thirteen Irish navvies were in custody for being engaged in the riot which ended in the murder of PC Pace.

Sheriff Spiers of Edinburgh later circulated details of two Irish labourers wanted for questioning in relation to the murder of Constable Richard Pace, and a reward of £50 (almost £5,000 today) was offered for information leading to their apprehension. The two suspects, who had left the area after the murder, were named as Patrick (Pat) Reilly and Peter Clark.

Even prior to this incident taking place, tensions had been running high between the Irish and Scottish labourers engaged in the building of the Hawick branch line. Just three days earlier on the 4 March, an Irish labourer by the name of Hughes was drinking in a public house in Pathhead when he started an argument with a Scottish labourer from Hawick. The other drinkers requested Hughes to leave the public house due to his drunken behaviour. After some difficulty, they persuaded Hughes to leave, but he returned a short time later with an open knife in his hand and stabbed the Scottish labourer inflicting serious injury. Hughes was subsequently arrested and taken into custody.

In the aftermath of these riots, meetings were held between railway officials and contractors. Wilson & Moore were the contractors who employed the Irish navvies and Graham & Sandison were responsible for employing the Scottish and English navvies. Agreements were eventually reached for both sets of workers to return to work. The two men, Patrick Reilly and Peter Clark, who were thought to have carried out the brutal murder of PC Pace were never seen or heard of again.

On 12 May, nine of the Scots and English contract workers named McQueen, McKillop, McLean, Grant, MacKay, McCracken, Morrison, Shaw and Henry Brown, appeared before the High Court in Edinburgh, charged with mobbing and rioting, fire-raising, malicious mischief and assault. The charges against McLean were dismissed. The other accused were all convicted and sentenced to terms of imprisonment ranging from eight months for Shaw to two years for Henry Brown.

In June that year, four Irish navvies appeared before the High Court in Edinburgh. They were all convicted in taking part in the first riot which led to the murder of Constable Pace. Lord Justice Clerk sentenced each of the men to seven years transportation. Construction work continued on the Edinburgh to Hawick branch line, which was completed without any further serious disruption, and it opened just three years later in 1849. The line continued in operation for 120 years until it was closed in 1969.

Macabre Contents of a Pine Box

On Sunday, 29 October 1848, Mr Watson, a passenger from Exeter in Devon was travelling on the GWR. Whilst waiting to catch a train at Slough Railway Station he saw a pine box unattended on the station platform. He drew the matter to the attention of a railway porter. The box did not appear to belong to anyone on the station, so the porter treated it as lost property. The box was held at Slough Station for several weeks but remained unclaimed.

The lost property regulations on the GWR at the time stipulated that any lost property found anywhere upon the railway and subsequently unclaimed, must be forwarded to the main lost property at Paddington Station where it would be retained for a minimum of twelve months before being disposed of by public auction. Consequently, the box in question was forwarded from Slough Station to the main lost property office at Paddington.

The procedure adopted at Paddington in relation to lost property forwarded to them was that a full examination of all lost property which had been on hand for over twelve months would be carried out on an annual basis. Only after that inspection, and if the owner could not be traced, was property to be sold by public auction. As a result of these procedures, the pine box remained in the lost property office at Paddington for some seventeen months after it had been found, before being examined with a view to its disposal.

On Saturday, 1 June 1850, Mr Bailey, the supervisor in charge of the lost property department at Paddington, was engaged in the disposal of lost property. Amongst the items of property to be disposed of was the wooden box found on Slough Station some seventeen months earlier. Upon opening the box Mr Bailey made a gruesome discovery. To his horror, he found the mutilated body of what appeared to be a young child wrapped in a piece of calico. Mr Bailey immediately reported the matter to Mr Seymour, General Manager of the GWR, who in turn contacted Superintendent Collard, the Chief of the GWR police, who attended the scene and immediately launched a murder investigation.

On Tuesday, 4 June 1850 an inquest was held at the Lord Hill public house in North Wharf Road, Paddington, presided over by the Middlesex (Western Division) Coroner, Mr Wakley. Evidence was given as to the finding of the unattended box on Slough railway station. The box was described as made of deal (pine) which measured approximately 14 inches (35.5 cm) square and 10½ inches (26.6 cm) deep. The box had been sewn up inside a piece of canvas.

Further evidence was given as to the transportation of the box by train to the Paddington Station lost property office where it had remained untouched until it was opened by Mr Bailey, who discovered the body which it was stated was carefully wrapped in a piece of calico. The body had all the appearances of a mummy, having been evidently pressed down in the box. A cambric handkerchief was tied tightly around its throat. There were cuts about the arms and legs, which appeared to show that attempts had been made to sever all the limbs from the body.

Doctor Thorne, a surgeon from Harrow Road, Paddington, gave evidence that the body was covered with flannel clothing. There were four teeth in the upper jaw and two teeth in the lower jaw. Dr Thorne found two deep cuts close together over the shoulder joint of the right arm, which in his opinion indicated that a blundering attempt had been made to remove the arm at the socket by someone unacquainted with anatomical principles. He further stated that the left arm and both thighs had been cut in a similar manner. The body was so horribly mutilated that its sex could not be ascertained. The sexual structure was completely removed. Dr Thorne formed the opinion that at the time of death, the child was between fifteen and eighteen months old. He had not the slightest doubt that the cause of death was due to strangulation.

The Coroner, Mr Wakley announced his verdict as wilful murder by some person or persons unknown. The coroner directed Superintendent Collard not to relax his exertions to discover the guilty parties, which he promised to do. Superintendent Collard did continue to investigate the murder, but he had little or no chance of ever solving the case. At that time, forensic science was unheard of. Basic blood grouping techniques would not be discovered for over half a century, and the method of fingerprinting was some forty years away from being adopted. It could not even be established whether the victim was a boy or a girl, and the murder itself, had been committed more than eighteen months before the remains of the body were discovered.

Although this case was never solved, Joseph Collard had a very successful career and solved many cases. He continued to work as Chief of Police for the GWR until his retirement in 1860 at the age of sixty. Several references to him can be found in old newspaper articles written at the time.

Chapter 2

Mid-Nineteenth Century

Murder, Manslaughter or Accident?

On Tuesday, 18 January 1853, Mrs Caroline Duffill, aged 37, the wife of Thomas Duffill, the landlord of the Freemason's Arms, Beverley, Yorkshire, left home just before midday and travelled to Hull by train. The main purpose of her visit was to collect some money which she was owed. For some reason, she never received the money but spent the afternoon in Hull before returning home on the last train which departed at 6.50 pm.

Mrs Duffill joined the train and she sat in a second-class compartment together with several other passengers. The train then proceeded to Cottingham, arriving at approximately 7 pm. Most of the passengers alighted from the compartment, leaving Mrs Duffill alone with just one other male passenger. When the train departed Cottingham for Beverley it was dark outside and just as the train started to leave the station, shouts and screams were heard coming from the compartment where she was sitting. The compartment door was flung open, and Mrs Duffill was either thrown, pushed or jumped from the train. Station staff who were standing on the platform saw her fall out of the carriage as the train left the station. They hurried off the end of the platform onto the track where they found her lying unconscious alongside the railway line.

The alarm was raised and Dr Watson, a local doctor, was summoned. He attended the scene, and Mrs Duffill was carried to the nearby Railway Tavern Hotel. Documents on her person revealed her identity, and arrangements were made for a message to be sent to the Freemason's Arms at Beverley to inform her husband about the incident. Mrs Duffill remained in a coma for six days until she eventually died of her injuries shortly after 8 am, on Monday, 24 January 1853.

Returning to the incident itself, after the train in question had left Cottingham, it continued towards Beverley. As the train slowed down on its approach to the station, a man was seen to jump from the compartment from which Mrs Duffill had fallen. He ran across a field and fled the scene.

An investigation ensued and William Holliday, aged 31, a local dairy farmer, was subsequently arrested. He admitted meeting Mrs Duffill in Hull on the afternoon in question and having several drinks with her before catching the last train home to Beverley. He stated that he may have travelled in the same compartment as Mrs Duffill but could not remember because he was drunk. He further stated that the only thing he remembered about the journey home was someone shouting 'Cottingham' whilst he was on the train. Holliday was subsequently conveyed to York Prison where he was remanded in custody on suspicion of having attacked Mrs Duffill.

The incident was widely reported in the media, showing headlines such as 'robbery and murder'. The events which took place were embellished by some newspapers who reported that a man had attacked and robbed Mrs Duffill of a substantial sum of money, before throwing her out of the compartment whilst the train was in motion, in order to silence her and avoid apprehension.

On Monday, 24 January an inquest was opened at the Beverley Arms. The presiding coroner was Mr E.D. Conyers.

Thomas Duffill gave evidence confirming that his wife Caroline left home at about 11.45 am on the day in question to travel to Hull by train. He did not see her again until about 10 pm the same evening after he had been called to the Railway Tavern where his wife was in a state of unconsciousness. He took her home the following morning where she remained until her death. She never recovered sufficiently to tell her husband what had happened. He could not say how much money was in her possession on her journey back from Hull. After Mr Duffill formally identified his wife's body, the inquest was adjourned until the following Friday.

On Friday 28 January, the inquest resumed. Mr Moss, a solicitor, was present on behalf of the Railway Company, and Mr Greaves, solicitor represented the accused, William Holliday.

Dr Samuel Watson gave evidence of being called to examine Mrs Duffill who was lying alongside the railway line unconscious after apparently falling from a train. He stated that she was suffering from cuts and bruises to her face, and blood was flowing from her nose. He was fully satisfied that she was suffering from concussion to the brain, and he arranged for her to be taken to the nearby Railway Tavern, and left instructions for her not to be moved that night. He further stated that her breath did smell of spirits, but he could not say how much alcohol she had consumed.

Dr Sandwith gave further medical evidence of seeing Mrs Duffill the morning after the incident when he had occasion to examine her. She was still in a state of unconsciousness and suffering from concussion and compression of the brain. Her face was swollen, and several cuts and abrasions were present. She also had a black eye. After her death, Dr Sandwith carried out a post mortem, but he did not find it necessary to cut open her body, as there was no doubt in his mind that the injuries to her head and brain resulted in her death.

William Brigham, a passenger in the next compartment to Mrs Duffill stated that he heard a woman screaming as the train left Cottingham, and later, as the train slowed down on approaching Beverley, he saw a man jump from the moving train before it arrived at the station.

Stephen Matthews the guard of the train deposed.

I am a guard with the York and Midland Railway Company and worked the last train on the night of the eighteenth. There was the engine, the tender, guard's van and five carriages. We arrived at Cottingham at two minutes past seven. I got out of my van and shouted out 'Cottingham' along the whole length of the train, before picking up a parcel for Beverley. I got onto the foot-board of my van as it was leaving the platform. I should point out that it would have been forty or fifty yards from my guards-van to the carriage where the deceased was, and I saw nothing of the accident. I knew nothing about it until the next morning. I did not hear her screams and would not have heard her, even if she had shouted out loudly. No passenger in any carriage can communicate with the guard.

Communication cords and similar devices had not been introduced to trains in 1853 so there was nothing anyone could have done to alert railway staff. The coroner, addressing Mr Locking, a railway official who was present, said this showed how necessary it was that something should be done in order that passengers might be enabled to communicate with the guard. Mr Locking replied he had no doubt something would be done in the near future.

Mr William Phillips deposed:

I am the Station-Master at Cottingham. I recollect the train coming in on the eighteenth. When the train departed, I was on the end of the platform near the last carriage. I did not hear or see anything wrong until the porter told me that a woman had jumped out of the carriage, and he was going for a doctor. I went along the track to the deceased, and a young man was holding her head. Doctor Watson came up, and she was removed to the Railway Tavern in Cottingham. Mrs Duffill had a purse in her possession which was handed to Mr Hawker at the Railway Tavern.

The purse was produced by a Mr Hawker at the inquest and contained £3 10s in gold, and 6/6d in silver (approximately £360 today).

Station Master Phillips; in answer to a question by a juryman said,'I feel quite confident the door was shut when the train left Cottingham Station'.

Mr Duffill said, in answer to questions by the coroner, 'I have no reason whatsoever to believe that any money was missing from my wife's person, and I do not believe she was robbed'

Detective Constable Charles Swift gave evidence relating to the arrest of William Holliday:

The prisoner asked me what I wanted with him, and I told him I wanted to ask him a question or two respecting Mrs Duffill. I asked him if he was at Hull on Tuesday, and he said he was. He said that he met with the deceased on Tuesday, and they had some drinks together in the afternoon. I asked him if he caught the same train as Mrs Duffill that night, and he said, 'Yes we had a glass of brandy and water together at the railway refreshment room'. I asked him if he came back in the same carriage with her. He said he might have done, but he could not say, because he was not very fresh. He did not recollect anything about the train journey other than the calling out of 'Cottingham'. He said he was partly asleep. I told him that he was being apprehended for throwing Mrs Duffill out of the carriage. He said, 'O dear I don't think I could ever do anything of the kind, but I was so drunk that I can't recollect anything about it'. That was all the conversation which passed.

The coroner in summing up said he did not believe Holliday intended to rob the deceased. It was his opinion that Holliday, if he had done anything at all, had attempted to commit an indecent assault upon her, which, if it had caused her to jump out of the train, meant that he would be guilty of manslaughter. The jury did return a verdict of manslaughter against William Holliday who was committed to stand trial at York Assizes, but the indictment against him was later dismissed due to lack of evidence.

The body of Mrs Caroline Duffill was interred at Beverley Minster, with a large crowd at the service.

Like numerous other crimes committed in the early Victorian era, it was often extremely difficult for the police to obtain sufficient evidence to secure a conviction. There was no DNA, blood grouping or forensic science which we all take for granted today. Evidence was in the main provided by eyewitness accounts and confessions. The full circumstances surrounding the tragic death of Caroline Duffill will never be known but the most likely scenario is that Mrs Duffill jumped from the train to avoid the advances of a drunken man, although without her testimony, securing a manslaughter conviction against William Holliday was an unlikely event.

Not long after this case, the first passenger communication cords were installed in new passenger train coaches. These early devices rang a warning bell inside the cab of the locomotive to attract the attention of the train driver. It did however take another fifteen years before legislation was introduced in 1868 to make these devices compulsory on all passenger trains.

Stabbed with a Butcher's Knife

Alfred Buckler was employed as a draper's assistant and lived in Poplar, East London. At about 8 pm on Thursday, 5 March 1857, Buckler went to Stepney Railway Station to catch a train to Hampstead. He purchased a second-class ticket and boarded an empty compartment on the train. Upon arrival at Camden Town Station, a young man by the name of William Webb opened the compartment door and got in. Webb sat opposite Buckler and opened a conversation by asking the name of the next station. Buckler informed him it was Hampstead Road. Webb then asked Buckler the time. Buckler took out his pocket-watch and said it was almost twenty-five-past-eight. Buckler then put the watch back in his pocket and turned his head to look out of the window.

Almost immediately, Buckler felt a violent blow on the back of his neck. He had in fact been stabbed. He turned around and saw Webb holding a knife in his left hand. Buckler sprang to his feet but felt a sharp pain in his left arm as Webb stabbed him again. Buckler then seized hold of Webb and started to grapple with him, blood flowing from his neck and arm. To prevent further stabbings, Buckler grabbed hold of the blade of the knife with his right hand, whilst he used his left hand to grab hold of Webb's right wrist, push it up against his throat and pin him into a corner. Buckler shouted out 'murder, murder' to attract the attention of passenger in adjoining carriages. Webb attempted to withdraw the knife from Buckler's hand, and although the knife cut deeper into his skin, Buckler refused to let go of the knife.

Eventually the train slowed down before coming to a halt at Hampstead Road Station. Buckler continued shouting, whilst pinning Webb into the corner of the carriage and eventually, the carriage door was opened by William Sandford, a railway porter. Webb immediately let go of the knife and said, 'The knife doesn't belong to me. This man tried to stab me and in self-defence I stabbed him.' Buckler then handed the knife over to the porter.

It was later established by police that William Webb was employed as a butcher, and the knife used in the attack was butcher's dressing knife, of the type used by Webb at work.

The Station Master and the train guard were quickly on the scene. Police were summoned and Webb was arrested on suspicion of attempted murder. Buckler was assisted to the Station Master's house for medical treatment. Mr Stephen Halford, a local doctor, was summoned and arrived soon afterwards. He examined Buckler, who was covered in blood and suffering from shock. Stab wounds were found on his neck just below his left ear and others were found close to the carotid artery. The wounds were each about 1 inch (2.54cm) long and 1 inch deep. There was a similar wound on the outer part of his left arm about 2 inches (5 cm) deep. It was the opinion of Doctor Halford that all these wounds were caused by stabbings and that a great deal of force must have been used to inflict them. There was also a cut on Buckler's forehead and his hands were lacerated and bleeding profusely. Doctor Halford administered treatment to all the wounds.

William Webb subsequently appeared before Marylebone Magistrates charged with attempting to murder Albert Buckler and he was committed to the Central Criminal Court (Old Bailey) to stand trial.

On Thursday, 9 April 1857, William Webb alias Philip Cohen, alias Philip Neavy, a butcher aged 19, appeared before the Central Criminal Court, charged with the felonious stabbing and wounding of Alfred Buckler with intent to murder him, and (second count) with intent to cause grievous bodily harm. He pleaded not guilty on both counts. Mr Sleigh QC represented Webb and Mr Payne QC appeared for the prosecution.

At the conclusion of the trial, the jury retired to consider their verdict. The jury later returned and delivered a not guilty verdict on the charge of attempted murder, but a unanimous guilty verdict on the second count of unlawful wounding with intent to commit grievous bodily harm. After the verdict was announced, the judge said that in all his experience, the prisoner's offence was one of the very worst he had ever met with, and he would be guilty of a very great dereliction of duty to the public if he did not pass the severest sentence the law permitted.

William Webb was subsequently sentenced to transportation to a penal colony beyond the seas for the term of his natural life. The prisoner portrayed no surprise at the sentence.

The First Railway Passenger Murder

On Saturday, 9 July 1864, Thomas Briggs, aged 69, a chief bank clerk who worked for Robarts' Bank in the City of London, went to Fenchurch Street Station on the North London Railway, to catch a train to Hackney where he lived. He was returning home after visiting his niece Caroline Buchan, who lived in Peckham, South-East London.

Upon arrival at Fenchurch Street Station, Briggs boarded the 9.50pm train and sat in an empty first-class compartment. This was later confirmed by a ticket collector who recognised him as a regular passenger. The train departed Fenchurch Street on time and after making scheduled intermediate stops at Bow and Hackney Wick stations, arrived at Hackney Station some twenty minutes later.

When the train arrived at Hackney, two young men boarded it and sat in an empty first-class compartment. It later transpired that the compartment they had entered was the same one that Briggs had occupied when the train left Fenchurch Street. After the two men entered the compartment, they noticed a bloodstained hat on the floor, and under one of the seats they found a small black bag and a bloodstained walking cane. They also noticed what appeared to be bloodstains on one of the windows, on the compartment floor, and on one of the seats. The men then summoned the train guard, Benjamin Aimes, who contacted Mr Greenwood, the Station Master at Chalk Farm Station (later re-named Primrose Hill until its closure in 1992) by telegraph. Station Master Greenwood replied that Aimes should lock the compartment in question and let the train proceeded to Chalk Farm where he would meet it, which he did, accompanied by police. The compartment in question was unlocked and the bloodstained items were removed and taken away by the policemen.

Meanwhile, at about 10.20pm that same evening, an empty train, travelling on the North London Railway in the opposite direction, had passed through Hackney Wick Station (also known as Victoria Park) travelling towards Bow when the driver noticed a dark object lying alongside the railway line. He shut off steam and applied the brakes of his locomotive until the train came to a halt. He then, together with the train guard, walked back along the track where they discovered a man lying next to the railway line. He was covered in blood, and barely alive. The train guard hurried to the Mitford Arms, a nearby public house and summoned assistance. The injured man was carried into the Mitford Arms pub where Police Constable Edward Dougan, the local policeman, was summoned to take charge of the situation.

Dr Brereton, a local doctor, was called out to treat the injured man and when he arrived, the man had already lapsed into unconsciousness. It appeared that he had received a severe beating with a blunt instrument to the head (probably by his own walking cane which was recovered from under the seat inside the train compartment). Dr Brereton also formed the opinion that the man was on the brink of death and unlikely to survive his injuries. The victim was later identified as Thomas Briggs. He never regained consciousness and died less than twenty-four hours later.

A murder enquiry was quickly underway and the evidence suggested that an unknown assailant entered the first-class compartment of the train which was already occupied by Briggs. He must have boarded the train either at Fenchurch Street before the train departed, or when the train stopped at Bow which was the next station. Briggs was then viciously assaulted and beaten over the head before being thrown from the train between Bow and Hackney Wick whilst it was in motion. This was supported by marks on his skin, consistent with being propelled along the track ballast, causing severe grazing and scuffing on his face and various parts of his body. It appears that the assailant had left the train at Hackney Wick, as he was not in the compartment when the train arrived at the next station, Hackney.

It was later established that the black bag and the walking cane recovered from under the seat of the empty compartment had belonged to Briggs. However, the bloodstained hat found in the compartment did not belong to him, and it was assumed that it was accidentally left behind by his assailant. As for the motive of the crime, Thomas Briggs was carrying a considerable amount of cash on his person, which was still intact inside one of his pockets after his body was discovered, which indicated that the assailant did not appear to have been after his money. However, Briggs was also known to have been in possession of an expensive gold pocket watch and fob-chain which was stolen from him. It seemed logical to assume therefore that the motive for the attack was one of robbery, in order to steal his gold watch and chain.

This first ever murder of a train passenger in Britain quickly made sensational news headlines in all the British newspapers. Posters were exhibited around the capital showing a picture of the bloodstained hat found at the scene of the crime, asking if any member of the public could recognise it. Substantial cash rewards were offered by the North London Railway Company, the government and Robarts' Bank for information leading to the arrest and conviction of the perpetrator of this terrible crime, and a nationwide manhunt for the culprit was underway.

A breakthrough in the investigation came when George Death, a jeweller with a shop at Cheapside in the City of London, reported to police that on

Monday 11 July 1864, just two days after the murder, a man walked into his shop and offered to sell him a gold fob-chain. They could not agree on a price so instead, Mr Death accepted the fob-chain in exchange for a cheaper necklace-chain and a ring which the man said were a gift for a young lady. George Death put the ring and chain in a jewellery case bearing the name of his shop. Death handed the gold fob-chain which he had received in the exchange over to the police. It was quickly confirmed that the fob-chain was in fact the chain which had been attached to the gold pocket watch stolen from Thomas Briggs during the robbery. The jeweller was only able to describe the man who gave him the gold chain as being a short man in his mid-twenties and thin build. He was almost certain however, that the man was foreigner, due to him having a distinct heavy foreign accent. Details of this new development was quickly circulated around the capital.

A spectacular new development in the enquiry occurred on 18 July when Jonathan Matthews, a horse-drawn cab driver from Paddington walked into his local police station and asked if he might examine the hat which had been widely circulated on posters in London, as it seemed familiar to him. After examining the hat, he positively identified it as one he had once given to a young German who had been a lodger at his house in Earl Street, Spitalfields in East London. Matthews told police that the man he gave the hat to was Franz Muller, a 23-year-old German immigrant who had been in England for about two years. Matthews went on to say that Muller had recently been courting his daughter. He was able to tell police that Muller, who was employed as a tailor, was currently lodging at an address in Park Terrace. Matthews then produced a jewellery box bearing the name 'Death's Jewellers, Cheapside'. Inside the box was a chain and a ring. Matthews said that Muller had given the items to his daughter as a gift because he was emigrating to America. George Death the jeweller, later confirmed to police that the box containing the ring and chain was the one he exchanged with the man who visited his shop with the gold fob-chain which was later identified as being stolen from Thomas Briggs.

Police then visited an address in Park Terrace where they spoke to Mrs Ellen Blyth, Muller's landlady who informed them that Muller had left the household on 14 July, and she had not seen or heard from him since. Further police enquiries revealed that Muller had in fact already emigrated from England on a sailing ship *The Victoria*, which had set sail for New York on the 15 July.

On 19 July 1864, Police obtained a warrant from Bow Street Magistrates Court for the arrest of Franz Muller in connection with the murder of Thoms Briggs. Police Inspector Richard Tanner and Police Sergeant George Clarke booked a passage on an express steamship to New York. They crossed the Atlantic on board the SS *City of Manchester* which departed on 22 July and arrived in New York on 5 August, two whole weeks before Muller was due to arrive there. Inspector Tanner liaised with the police in New York City and when the sailing ship *The Victoria* arrived in New York Harbour, Muller was immediately placed under arrest. The only luggage he was carrying was a small box, inside which police recovered a few personal items, including the gold pocket watch which had been stolen from Thomas Briggs. Muller was taken before the authorities in New York where an extradition order was issued and police escorted Muller back to England. They arrived at Liverpool Docks on 16 September 1864 where they were met by crowds of excited people who jeered as Muller was escorted from the vessel by Inspector Tanner and Sergeant Clark. Muller was escorted from Liverpool to London by train where they were greeted with hoots and boos by masses of people who had congregated at Euston Station to witness their arrival.

On 24 October, the trial of Franz Muller began at the Old Bailey. The judge was Mr Baron Martin. Muller was represented by an eminent lawyer Mr Parry who had been engaged and funded by the German Legal Protection Society in London who often funded cases involving German citizens. The prosecution was conducted by the Solicitor General Mr Ballantine.

Muller pleaded not guilty to the wilful murder of Thomas Briggs, and he remained cool and collected throughout the trial. During the trial, the defence argued that the case against Muller was purely circumstantial. It was stated that the prosecution had not produced a single witness to show that Muller was at Fenchurch Street, Bow or Hackney Wick Stations, or that he travelled by train on the day of the murder. There were no bloodstains on his clothing which he was wearing when arrested. Muller denied travelling by train and said that at the time of the murder he was visiting a prostitute in Camberwell. With regards to the gold pocket watch stolen from Thomas Briggs and found in his possession when he arrived in New York, Muller stated that he bought it cheap from a man on the docks in London and thought it may have been stolen so he traded the fob-chain for the ring and necklace chain at the jewellers in London and kept the watch for himself.

The trial against Franz Muller lasted less than three days and at 2.30pm on 27 October 1864, the third day of the trial, the jury retired to consider their verdict. It took them just fifteen minutes to deliberate, before returning a unanimous verdict of guilty to the charge of wilful murder. After hearing the verdict, Muller burst into tears and cried as the judge passed the mandatory sentence of death by hanging.

On Monday 14 November 1864, a large noisy crowd, estimated at 50,000 people, gathered outside Newgate Prison in London to witness the execution. Many of the spectators had been drinking heavily and some were drunk. Amongst the onlookers, both men and women were dirty vagrants, ruffians and members of the poorest classes of Victorian society as well as young gentlemen and people of the upper and middle-classes.

At 7.45am, church bells began to sound, and Muller was escorted up the steps of the gallows. His wrists were strapped in front of him, and his arms were strapped to his waist by a leather belt. Just before 8am, William Calcraft, the executioner, placed the noose around his neck before hooking the other end of the rope onto a chain hanging from the beam. Calcraft then pulled a white hood over the head of Muller who was asked by a German speaking priest if he wished to confess to his crime. It is alleged that he replied in German 'Yes, I did it.' The priest supposedly replied in German, 'Christ have mercy upon you soul.' The scaffold bolt was released by the executioner and Muller dropped a short distance. His body quivered momentarily before becoming still. His body was later removed from the scaffold and interred within the precinct of Newgate Prison.

The execution of Franz Muller was one of the last public hangings to take place in Britain. Just four years later in 1868, the Capital Punishment (Amendment) Act was passed which abolished public executions and all future judicial hangings were carried out inside prison walls and not witnessed by any members of the public.

Station Master Shot by a Railway Porter

During the 1860s, Edward Adolphus James Walsh was employed by the London, Chatham & Dover Railway Company as a Station Master at Dover Priory Railway Station. He was a quiet inoffensive man, well liked and highly respected within the local community.

He was the most senior railway official at the railway station and the person in charge of all other staff members which included bookings clerks, railway porters, signalmen, ticket collectors and shunters.

One of his staff members was a young 18-year-old railway porter by the name of Thomas Wells who was unpopular amongst most of his works colleagues due to his aggressive manner, lack of discipline and bad behaviour, which Station Master Walsh had addressed with him on several occasions.

In the spring of 1867, Thomas Wells started carrying a pistol with him when he came to work. He used it to shoot at objects both outside and sometimes inside the station buildings whilst he was working. Other members of staff soon began to complain to Station Master Walsh about Wells firing the pistol whilst at work. Walsh again warned Wells about his behaviour and said that he must refrain from firing his pistol whilst he was in work. Wells took no notice and carried on firing the pistol whilst on duty.

The Station Master was left with no alternative, other than report him to the railway company management, with a view to disciplinary proceedings to be instituted against him. As a result, Mr Cox, a senior official of the railway company, visited Dover Priory Railway Station on Wednesday, 1 May and spoke to Porter Wells in the presence of Station Master Walsh in the Station Master's Office. Cox told Wells that he must apologise to Station Master Walsh for his bad behaviour, and he must also promise not to discharge his pistol again whilst on duty, otherwise he faced dismissal from the railway. Wells then became infuriated and enraged at having been reported by Station Master Walsh. In order to calm down the situation, Mr Cox told Walsh that he would not press him for an immediate answer, but he should go outside for ten minutes, calm down and think about it, which he did. After the allotted time, Wells was summoned back into the office. He was once again asked to apologise to the Station Master for his conduct, but he refused to do so. Mr Cox then told Porter Wells that due to his attitude, lack of discipline and unacceptable behaviour, he would be submitting a full report on the matter recommending that he should face a fine or dismissal from the service for misconduct.

Mr Cox then left the Station Master's Office, and as he walked along the station platform, he heard a loud bang. He turned around and saw Wells running out of the office with a pistol in his hand. He watched as Wells jumped from the station platform onto the railway line and ran towards some carriages which were stabled in nearby railway sidings. Mr Cox went back the Station Master's Office and found Station Master Walsh lying on the floor, having been shot through the head at point blank range. He appeared to be dead.

Police were summoned and Mr Cox directed officers to the railway sidings where they eventually found Wells hiding in a railway carriage He was arrested by police, who seized the pistol which was still in his possession.

Thomas Wells was subsequently charged with the wilful murder of Edward Walsh. His trial took place at Maidstone Assizes on 23 July 1868 before Mr Justice Willes. He pleaded not guilty to the charge and his defence lawyer Mr Ribton asked the jury to acquit the prisoner of murder and find him guilty of manslaughter. He told the jury that he was not suggesting that his client was insane, but his unpredictable behaviour was due to brain damage resulting from a severe bang on the head received by his client who was struck by a moving wagon during an accident whilst at work.

The jury had earlier been told that there was no record of any such accident having taken place. There was nothing recorded in the station accident register, and no other staff members were aware of any accident involving Wells and he had never mentioned anything about an accident to any of his works colleagues.

In his summing up, however, the Judge told the jury that it was not part of his duty to interpret the speech of the learned counsel for the prisoner, but it was his duty to inform them of the law in this country relating to murder, which was that every man who deliberately killed another was guilty of the crime of murder and they must either find the prisoner guilty of that offence, or acquit him altogether. He then outlined the full facts of the case before leaving it in the hands of the jury. The jury retired and deliberated for less than five minutes, before finding the prisoner Thomas Wells guilty of murder by a unanimous decision.

Mr Justice Willes donned his black cap before pronouncing the mandatory sentence of death by hanging. Wells showed no emotion as he left the dock.

On Thursday, 13 August Thomas Wells walked up the steps of the gallows inside Maidstone Prison. He was dressed in his railway uniform. It was the first private hanging execution in Britain, following a recent Act of Parliament, which abolished public executions and ordered that that capital punishment must be carried out within the prison walls. The prisoner prayed for a few moments with the prison chaplain, Reverend Fraser, before the execution was carried out by William Calcraft, the public executioner.

Following his trial, Thomas Wells did express remorse for his actions and wrote a letter to Mrs Walsh, the widow of his victim, begging her forgiveness. He fully acknowledged his guilt, and no efforts were made in any quarter to obtain a remission in the capital sentence.

Chapter 3

Late Nineteenth Century

Murder on the Brighton Line

On Monday, 27 June 1881, Frederick Gold, aged 64, a corn merchant who ran a business in Walworth, South London, caught the 2pm train from London Bridge Station to Brighton on the London, Brighton and South Coast Railway (LBSCR). He was a regular passenger on the Brighton line. He arrived at London Bridge Station wearing an expensive suit and carrying an umbrella. There, he boarded an empty first-class compartment and sat in a corner seat, facing the direction of travel. The train in question was a semi-fast train, which after leaving London Bridge only stopped at East Croydon and Preston Park Stations before arriving at Brighton. Just as the train was preparing to leave London Bridge, a young man opened the door and jumped into the same compartment as Gold. The young man looked at Frederick Gold, nodded and sat down on the seat in the opposite corner.

After departing London Bridge on time, the train stopped at East Croydon before continuing to Preston Park, arriving there about an hour later. Upon arrival at Preston Park, a 21-year-old man who later gave his name as Percy Mapleton Lefroy, staggered out of a first-class compartment covered in blood. He was very distressed and approached a ticket collector on the station platform. He told the ticket collector that he boarded the train at London Bridge and there were two other men in the same compartment. He further stated that as the train went through a railway tunnel between East Croydon and Preston Park, he was attacked and beaten by the two men who also tried to shoot at him with a gun but missed. The next thing he remembered was the train pulling in to Preston Park Station where he managed to alight. The Station Master then arrived on the scene and was informed of what had happened. The Station Master noticed what appeared to be a gold chain sticking out of one of the young man's boots and he asked what it was. The young man mumbled something about it being his gold watch which he had managed to conceal in his boot to prevent it being stolen by the two men. The Station Master then asked the man if he needed medical treatment, but he declined, saying that he would be alright. The Station Master then arranged for the man to be taken to the nearest police station where officers of the LBSCR Police would meet him to investigate his complaint further.

Upon arrival at the police station, Lefroy was met by Detective Sergeant George Holmes and another officer from the railway police. Lefroy repeated his earlier story, made to the ticket collector and the Station Master. DS Holmes pointed out to him that when he got off the train there was nobody else in the compartment from which he alighted. Lefroy stated that the men who attacked him must have jumped out just before the train stopped or perhaps made their way along the footboard to another compartment whilst the train was still in motion. Detective Sergeant Holmes also noticed a lot of blood on his clothing which did not appear to have come from any of the obvious injuries which Lefroy himself had sustained. Overall, DS Holmes was very sceptical about his story, but due to his injuries he decided to convey him to hospital for treatment. Lefroy was subsequently taken to the Sussex County Hospital. A few hours later, he was discharged from hospital, and he was taken back to Brighton Railway Station where DS Holmes was awaiting him, in order to verify his home address which he had earlier given police whilst being interviewed.

DS Holmers then escorted Lefroy by train to Wallington in Surrey where Lefroy said that he was living as a lodger in his sister's boarding house. Upon arrival at the house, Lefroy told Holmes that he needed to go upstairs to his room which he did. DS Holmes waited downstairs, but Lefroy never returned. He had in fact slipped out of the back door of the house and disappeared.

In the meantime, other detectives had been searching through the train on which Lefroy had travelled, which had been shunted into some railway sidings after completing its journey to Brighton. They found the first-class compartment where the alleged incident had taken place. There were what appeared to be heavy bloodstains on the seats and floor of the compartment, and two bullet-holes were found in one of the seat cushions. Bullets were recovered from each of the holes.

Whilst the examination of the train was being conducted in the railway sidings at Brighton, a search of the railway line itself was also being carried out between East Croydon and Preston Park Stations. One of the key areas of the search was Balcombe Tunnel, located about 17 miles (27km) north of Brighton. Later that day, during a search being conducted inside the tunnel, a gruesome discovery was made. The body of an old man was found which was later identified as that of Frederick Gold. He had been beaten about the head and viciously stabbed fourteen times which had caused his death. He had also been shot twice, although the shots themselves had not been fatal. His train season ticket was still in his pocket but a gold pocket watch and chain which he always carried had been stolen from his pocket. Not far from the body, a bloodstained knife was found which it was believed to be the murder weapon. Further along the line between Balcombe Tunnel and Preston Park, police found his umbrella, and not far away they found the revolver believed to have been used in the shooting.

On Wednesday, 29 June, an inquest was held into the death of Frederick Gold which lasted several days, after which the jury returned a verdict of 'wilful murder' by Percy Lefroy. A manhunt was quicky underway to find Lefroy and a detailed description of him appeared in all the daily newspapers. A composite picture of him was exhibited on wanted posters which were circulated nationwide, and on 8 July Lefroy was finally arrested after being found lodging under the name of Mr Park, in a squalid room of house at 32 Smith Street, Stepney, East London.

The trial of Percy Mapleton Lefroy (also known as Percy Lefroy Mapleton) later took place at Maidstone Assizes before Lord Chief Justice Coleridge. Lefroy pleaded not guilty to the wilful murder of Frederick Gold, but the evidence was overwhelming, and the jury took just ten minutes to return a guilty verdict. Percy Lefroy was hanged at Lewes Prison on 29 November. The executioner was William Marwood.

Attempt to Assassinate Queen Victoria

On 2 March 1882, Roderick MacLean was arrested after attempting to shoot Queen Victoria at Windsor Railway Station. The Queen had travelled from Paddington Station in London to Windsor Railway Station in Berkshire on the Royal Train. After alighting from the train, she walked to an awaiting horse-drawn carriage to be conveyed to Windsor Castle. As the carriage pulled away from the station, MacLean, who was standing amongst a crowd of public spectators, pulled out a pistol and fired a shot in the direction of the queen, before being apprehended. Fortunately, the shot narrowly missed its target, and the coach drove off at speed towards Windsor Castle, carrying her to safety. This had been the eighth (and final) attempt by different individuals to assassinate Queen Victoria during her reign.

Roderick MacLean subsequently appeared before Reading Assizes charged with High Treason. He was judged to be insane and after a five minute deliberation by the jury he was found 'not guilty' of High Treason by reason of insanity, and acquitted. MacLean was detained in Broadmoor Lunatic Asylum during Her Majesty's pleasure and spent the rest of his life confined to the Asylum until his death on 9 June 1921.

The outcome of this case prompted Queen Victoria herself to ask for a change in English Law to be made to enable a verdict of 'guilty but insane' to be handed out in future similar cases as opposed to the 'not guilty' verdict which had been delivered by the jury. A law which enabled this to happen was speedily passed through parliament, and the Trial of Lunatics Act 1883 came into force the following year.

Attempt to Assassinate a High Court Judge

Following the attempt to assassinate HRH Queen Victoria in 1882, another incident which involved the attempted assassination of a high-profile train passenger occurred less than a decade later. The target on that occasion was a high court judge.

At 5.40pm on Tuesday, 19 November 1889, Samuel Botelier Bristowe, a high court judge, was boarding a Great Northern Railway train at Nottingham, London Road Railway Station (closed in 1944), to travel to Derby. A railway official opened a first-class compartment door to allow the judge to board the train, and as Judge Bristowe stepped onto the running board of the coach, a man standing behind him pulled a revolver from his coat pocket and fired single shot at the judge from point- blank range. The bullet pierced the judge between the shoulder blades, causing damage to his lung. He was rushed to hospital where he remained in a critical condition for several weeks but fortunately, he survived the attack. Doctors were unable to remove the bullet and it remained lodged in his body until his death in 1897 at the age of 74.

Edward Wilhelm Hermann Arnemann, a German citizen, was arrested by police and admitted shooting the judge. He appeared before the Nottingham Assizes on 8 March 1890 where he pleaded guilty to attempted murder, before being sentenced to twenty years penal servitude.

The Fenian Bombing Campaign

The Fenian bombing campaign, also known as the Fenian dynamite campaign or the Fenian movement, was an Irish revolutionary campaign intended to overthrow the British rule of Ireland in the latter half of the nineteenth century. It went on to become the first organised sustained terrorist bombing campaign in Britain. The campaign, which took place between 1881 and 1898, was orchestrated, and carried out by Irish republican paramilitary groups on both government and civilian targets, including the railway network, causing widespread damage and destruction, as well as personal injuries and loss of life. These acts of terrorism were deemed to be criminal acts which included the offences of treason, murder, attempted murder, and manslaughter.

Bombings of the first railway targets occurred on the London Underground, when at 8pm on Tuesday, 30 October 1883, without warning, a colossal explosion occurred at Paddington Station after a bomb was thrown out of a first-class carriage of an eastbound Metropolitan line train. The massive explosion ripped through the tunnel causing considerable damage and mayhem on the network. Three carriages on the rear of the train from which the bomb was thrown were completely wrecked. By some miracle, nobody was killed by the blast but there were more than forty casualties who suffered injuries, some of which were serious. The underground was plunged into darkness, which hampered the emergency services who attended the scene.

A few minutes after the Paddington explosion, another blast occurred in a tunnel on the District Line, between Charing Cross and Westminster

Bridge Stations. Windows were blown out and considerable damage was caused to both railway stations which were approximately half a mile apart, and gas lamps on the platforms of both stations were extinguished, plunging them into darkness. Fortunately, there were no fatalities or serious injuries caused by the blast, but passengers on the station platform at Charing Cross, waiting to catch a westbound train due at 8.05pm were badly shaken. The infrastructure of the gas-lighting system was not affected by the explosion and the lamps were able to be re-lit almost immediately, and lighting was restored. It was believed that the explosives used in the blast were dropped down a ventilation shaft from the street above into the underground railway tunnel between the two stations.

On Friday, 4 January 1885, another explosion occurred in a tunnel on the Metropolitan Railway, this time near Charlton Street Underground Station located in the Euston Road at St Pancras. Just after 9pm in the evening, a westbound train was travelling through the tunnel when an explosive device containing dynamite was thrown from the train as it was passing an eastbound train. The bomb exploded almost immediately, causing considerable damage to the eastbound train. Almost all the windows along the entire length of the train were shattered by the explosion, and one of the doors was blown off. Remarkably, there were no fatalities, although several passengers on the train suffered injuries, mostly caused by flying glass. The blast could be heard and felt at King's Cross Underground Station, and in the streets above.

During the nineteenth century Fenian campaign, the explosions targeted at the London Underground railway network in 1883 and 1885 miraculously did not result in any fatalities, nevertheless, there were numerous casualties, some of whom suffered very serious injuries. Sadly, one fatality did occur when another Fenian terrorist explosion occurred at Aldersgate Underground Station (now called Barbican), on the Metropolitan Railway Circle line in 1897, which resulted in a murder enquiry being set up.

The incident occurred near the end of the evening rush-hour period, when at 7pm on Monday 26 April 1897, a crowded train from Farringdon Street entered Aldersgate Station. The station platform was full of passengers and, as the train came to a halt. a deafening explosion was heard, emanating from a first-class carriage in the centre of the train. It was later established that an explosive device had been placed beneath a seat on the train. There was widespread panic on the station and a general stampede of passengers. Glass fell from the station roof and the station was plunged into semi-darkness as the gas lights were extinguished by the blast.

The carriage in which the explosion occurred was completely wrecked and a carriage door was hurled across the station platform whilst other doors were partially torn from their hinges. Carriages on either side of the one where the explosion occurred were also completely wrecked and severe damage was caused to the rest of the train, with several windows being shattered. A portion of a London, Chatham, and Dover Company train, which was standing in another platform was also badly damaged. The explosion was such, that the blast was also heard as far away as Farringdon Street and Moorgate Street stations.

There were many people injured during the explosion and a considerable number of police officers, ambulance crews and railway officials were quickly on the scene. Within half an hour, at least ten people with serious injuries had been removed to St Bartholomew's Hospital, whilst first aid was being rendered to many other casualties on the train and station platforms. Roads outside the station were cordoned off and road traffic was suspended to non-emergency vehicles.

One of the casualties conveyed to St Bartholomew's was Henry Pitts, an engineer from Tottenham. Pitts was travelling in a carriage adjoining the one where the explosion occurred, and he received multiple injuries from which he died shortly after arriving at the hospital.

On Monday, 24 May 1897, a Coroner's enquiry into the death of Henry Pitts was concluded in London. Colonel Majendie of the Home Office confirmed that the explosion was caused by high explosives having been placed on the floor of the carriage. The jury returned a verdict of 'wilful murder by some person or persons unknown'. The culprit/s were never caught, and the case remains unsolved.

Robbery and Attempted Murder on the Metropolitan Railway

On the evening, on Saturday 21 August 1880, a young man named Clarence Lewis aged 18 who was employed by Messrs Barnham's, tea merchants of

Ravens Road, Spitalfields, East London, visited the premises of another branch of the firm located in Kensington, West London, to collect the cash takings for that week. After collecting £105 in cash (over £11,600 today), which was placed inside a paper bag, he walked to Kensington Railway Station to catch a train back to Spitalfields with the money. Upon his arrival at the station, he was approached by a stranger, Stephen Henry Perry, aged 24, of Duke Street, Marylebone. Perry, a well-dressed man, was a former employee of Messrs Barnham and as such familiar with the fact that a member of staff collected the weekly takings from the Kensington branch of the company on Saturday evenings to convey it to the 'head office' in Ravens Road in East London.

Perry, as a former employee of Barnham's, claimed old acquaintance and invited Lewis to travel with him in a first-class compartment, for which he offered to pay. Lewis accepted the invitation, and shortly before 11pm, they boarded a train together to travel towards the City. There were no other occupants in the compartment.

During the journey, Perry produced a bottle of port wine from his pocket and offered Lewis a drink, which Lewis accepted. Perry then offered him another beverage which Lewis tasted but did not like. As the train entered a tunnel after departing King's Cross Station, Perry attempted to subject Lewis to some chloroform, but Lewis pushed him away. Perry then attacked Lewis and started to beat him violently about the head with a stout walking cane, whilst at the same time kicking him about the body. Lewis was bleeding profusely, and the railway carriage was covered in blood. Perry dragged Lewis towards the carriage door, trying to open it whilst the train was in motion, in order to throw him out of the compartment, but Lewis continued to struggle with his assailant until finally, he lapsed into unconsciousness and slumped to the floor. Perry then stole the bag containing the money. The train then arrived at Aldersgate Street Station, where Perry alighted. Lewis who had briefly regained consciousness managed to stagger from the train and began shouting to attract the attention of station staff and other passengers. Perry started to flee the station, but he was apprehended by the station staff who detained him and summoned the police. Lewis, who had again relapsed into unconsciousness was conveyed to St. Bartholomew's Hospital in a serious condition. Clarence Lewis survived his attack but remained in hospital for three weeks before being discharged, still in a debilitated condition.

After his arrest by police, Perry was searched and his pockets were found to contain a bottle of port wine, a bottle of laudanum (alcoholic solution containing morphine), a bottle of chloroform and the paper bag containing the £105 in cash stolen from Lewis.

Stephen Henry Perry appeared before the Guildhall Magistrates Court in the City of London on Monday, 23 August, charged with robbery and attempted murder. He was remanded in custody.

On Wednesday, 15 September, Perry appeared before the Central Criminal Court in London charged with assault and wounding Clarence Lewis with intent to murder him or with intent to do grievous bodily harm (alternative charges). He was further charged with robbery upon the same person. The judge was Mr Justice Stephen. Mr Poland and Mr Montague prosecuted on behalf of the public prosecutor. Mr Grain and Mr Morris appeared for the defence. Perry pleaded not guilty on both counts.

The evidence conclusively proved that the defendant Perry was the person who attacked Lewis on the train and stole the money. Upon conclusion of the trial the jury immediately announced a unanimous verdict of guilty on the count of assault and wounding with intent to commit grievous bodily harm (not guilty of attempted murder), and guilty of robbery.

After the verdict was announced, Mr Grain addressed the court on behalf of Perry and endeavoured to show that the robbery was not premeditated but was as a result of sudden temptation. In rebuttal to this address, Mr Poland (prosecutor) called a young man named Emmett, an employee of Messrs Barnham, who had also occasionally carried the money from one establishment to the other, and he proved that on the previous Saturday when he was so engaged, the prisoner got into the same carriage with him and pressed him to a drink something from a bottle, but he refused.

The learned judge said he had no doubt that Perry had deliberately planned the robbery, and that he had used the most brutal violence to carry out that object. He said it was the most cowardly and brutal outrage that had ever been brought under his notice, and it was hardly possible to believe that a young man like the prisoner, who appeared to have possessed some respectability of position and a certain amount of education, could have been guilty of such a brutal and cowardly act. He had no doubt that after the prisoner had carried out his act of plunder, he had attempted to throw Lewis out of the carriage, utterly regardless of the consequences. Under all the circumstances he ordered him to receive thirty lashes of the cat-o'-nine-tails and penal servitude (imprisonment with hard labour) for twenty years. The prisoner uttered a scream when sentence was pronounced.

After sentencing Perry to thirty lashes, Mr Justice Stephen told him that it was done 'in order that, coward as you are, you may feel the pain and know what it means'. He went on to say that the brutality of crime would be lessened if floggings were invariably resorted to. Wife-beaters, maltreaters of policemen, and sturdy vagabonds, generally would be speedily reduced in numbers if they knew that detection would be followed not merely by a peaceful seclusion in gaol, but by excruciating pains in their own persons. Those who are most callous of the feelings of others are frequently most alive to pain. None but crimes of brutality should be punished in such a way. A codification of lashes according to the enormity of the offence would speedily bring about a respect for the limbs and lives of Her Majesty's subjects. Perry was removed from the dock.

The flogging of Stephen Henry Perry was administered at Newgate prison on Friday 1 October 1880.

Railway Policemen Shot by Thieves

Sometimes, police officers in uniform can become victims of crime merely by being in the wrong place at the wrong time. That is precisely what happened to Joseph Byrne, a Police Constable in the London and North Western Railway (LNWR) Police, who was shot dead when he approached a gang of men whilst performing duties in the tranquil village of Plumpton near Carlisle in Cumbria.

At about 8pm on Wednesday, 28 October 1885, shortly after dark, a ruthless gang of four professional jewel thieves from London known as the 'ladder gang' committed an audacious burglary at Netherby Hall, the home of Sir Frederick Graham and his wife, Lady Hermione. The hall was set in a 36 acre estate at Longtown near Carlisle. The gang gained access to the premises by using a ladder to scale the building, before entering an upstairs bedroom window whilst Sir Frederick and his wife were having dinner downstairs.

Having entered the building, the gang stole a quantity of jewellery which included three diamond stars and two pairs of diamond earrings from a jewellery case belonging to Lady Hermione. The items were valued at £250 (over £30,000 today).

As the men were about to steal more items of jewellery, they were disturbed by a household maid banging on the bedroom door which the men had locked from the inside. The maid ran downstairs and sounded the alarm that there were intruders on the premises. The men quickly escaped down the ladder and left the estate with the jewellery they had already stolen.

The local police were informed about the burglary and a search for the culprits was quickly underway. Police officers caught sight of the gang at nearby Kingstown and Sergeant Roche, accompanied by PC Johnson of the Cumbria Constabulary approached the men. A struggle ensued and both officers were savagely beaten with a metal crowbar. One of the men then produced a revolver and shot Sergeant Roche in the arm, before shooting PC Johnson in the chest. Another officer, PC Fortune, later tried to apprehend the men, but as he approached them, he was beaten unconscious with the metal crowbar. PC Fortune was rushed to hospital where it was established that he had received nineteen wounds to his skull. All three police officers eventually recovered from their injuries.

The gang members then headed in the direction of Dalton Road railway crossing before walking along the railway track. Fearing that the men would leave the area by train, police contacted a local railway Station Master and details of the gang were circulated to various railway stations and signal boxes by the railway telegraph system.

In the meantime, the gang had made their way to Plumpton Railway Station where at about 10pm, they enquired about train times to London. After being told that the last train had already gone, they started loitering in the vicinity of the station. Police Constable Joseph Byrne of the LNWR Police who was on duty there was alerted and bravely approached the men.

One of the men immediately pulled out a revolver and shot PC Byrne in the head. He was then thrown over a wall where he later died.

Three of the criminals then managed to board a goods train which was bound for Keswick, but they were spotted by a watchful train guard who arranged for a telegram to be sent to Tebay railway station, requesting that police meet the train upon its arrival there. When the train arrived in Tebay, the gang was confronted by an angry crowd of railway workers armed with sticks, shovels and other makeshift weapons who searched the train and found the men hiding beneath a tarpaulin covering one of the wagons. One of the men produced a revolver but was disarmed after being struck over the head with a piece of wood. A vicious struggle ensued but the men were grossly outnumbered by the infuriated rail workers who gave them a sound beating before the men were tied to telegraph poles to await the arrival of the police. When police officers did arrive, they recovered the stolen jewellery, two revolvers, and other weapons from the gang members. The three men were taken into custody by police. A fourth member of the gang, William Baker, who was not involved in the assaults and shootings that took place, was later arrested in Lancaster. He did not resist arrest and was subsequently sentenced to penal servitude for his part as an accomplice in the burglary at Netherby Hall.

The three main gang members, who were later named as Anthony Benjamin Rudge, John Martin and James Baker (no relation to William Baker, the fourth gang member), were taken before local magistrates, and remanded in custody until they appeared before Mr Justice Day at the Cumberland Assizes on 18 January 1886. They were charged with various offences, including the wilful murder of Police Constable Joseph Byrne, other serious assaults, and the burglary at Netherby Hall. The three men pleaded not guilty on all counts. The trial lasted for two days and on Wednesday, 20 January 1886, the jury retired to deliver their verdict. It took them just over one hour to deliver a guilty verdict on all charges, in respect of each of the three defendants.

The judge, Mr Justice Day, imposed the mandatory death sentence on the accused men and on Monday, 8 February sentence was carried out and the three prisoners were hanged at Carlisle Prison. They showed no remorse for the crimes they had committed, or for their victims.

Murder of a Victorian Railway Detective

On Sunday, 29 September 1895, Detective Constable William Henry Osborne of the LNWR Police, stationed at Wigan, was instructed to carry out night observations at the railway sidings near Chapel Lane, Wigan, due to the theft of goods which was taking place from the sheeted railway wagons stabled there. He was to be accompanied by Detective Sergeant Robert Kidd, who was stationed in Manchester. DS Kidd caught a train from Manchester and arrived in Wigan where he liaised with Osborne shortly before 8pm. Both men then made their way to the railway sidings by walking alongside the main railway line. Osborne led the way with Kidd following immediately behind him. After a while, they arrived in the vicinity of the sidings which was separated from the main railway line by a brick wall. It was shortly after dark. As they walked alongside the wall, the officers heard voices coming from the other side of it and when they got to the end of the wall, Osborne peered around the corner, and came face to face with a man. Osborne said to the man, 'Who are you? What are you up to?' The man replied, 'Who are you?' The man then started to run away but Constable Osborne caught hold of him and a struggle took place. Another man appeared on the scene and aided the man who was struggling with Osborne. Osborne was able to draw his truncheon, but one of the men grabbed hold of it. Osborne however had a firm grip on the leather strap and was able to swing it around like a flail, hitting one of the men. The two men continued to struggle with Osborne until he was badly beaten, overpowered and bundled to the ground before the men ran away.

In the meantime, whilst Osborne had been struggling with the two men, others had appeared out of the darkness, and DS Kidd was in a struggle of his own, after confronting two other men who then attacked him. Kidd however was not so lucky. One of his assailants pulled out a knife, and in a frenzied attack, stabbed him nine times around the face, neck and chest. Kidd collapsed to his knees in a pool of blood. His attackers ran away and made good their escape.

DC Osborne eventually got to his feet and approached Sergeant Kidd who was on his hands and knees nearby. Osborne assumed Kidd had been kicked about the head, as blood was flowing profusely from wounds on his head and face. Kidd said, 'Is that you Osborne?' Osborne replied, 'Yes.' Kidd said, 'Get me a drink of water.' Osborne then attempted to carry Kidd to safety but after struggling a few yards he had to lie him down beneath a wagon. It was there that Sergeant Kidd died due to his stab wounds and loss of blood. Dr Graham from Wigan later examined the body and pronounced life extinct.

In the meantime, Detective Constable Osborne, badly beaten and completely exhausted, managed to crawl to a nearby signal box where he raised the alarm before losing consciousness. An ambulance was summoned, and he was taken to hospital. Detective Chief Inspector Richards of the LNWR Police was contacted, and he attended the scene, accompanied by detectives Davern and Buckingham. A murder investigation was soon underway.

Local police who were also informed of the incident attended, but initially there was some confusion as to the police force, in whose jurisdiction the railway sidings were located. Chapel Lane sidings were on the border of two neighbouring police authorities, the Wigan Borough Police, and the Lancashire County Constabulary. Both police forces quickly responded to the request for assistance. Superintendent Brassington of the Lancashire Constabulary attended, having in the region of forty officers at his disposal.

Superintendent Macintosh, who in the absence of the Chief Constable, Captain Bell, was in overall command of the Wigan Borough Constabulary, was the first officer on the scene, taking as many officers with him as he could muster. It was quickly established that the exact spot in which the murder of DS Kidd had taken place was in fact within the jurisdiction of the Wigan Borough Constabulary. It was decided however, that as Superintendent Brassington and his officers were already a part of the investigation, he would continue to assist the LNWR Police, and the Wigan Borough Constabulary wherever possible.

The Wigan Borough Police under the direction of Superintendent Macintosh, began house to house enquiries starting in Kay's Houses, a cluster of cottages adjacent to Chapel Lane railway sidings, separated from the sidings by a wall and a wooden fence. It was well known to local officers that several railway thieves lived in these cottages, and they had in the past been frequently responsible for pilfering railway wagons berthed in the sidings. Searches were carried out by police in several of the properties. Similar enquires and searches were conducted at houses in nearby Spring View, which contained other residents who were well known to the police.

During these house-to-house enquiries, a total of five men were arrested by Superintendent Macintosh and his officers, on suspicion of being concerned in the wilful murder of Sergeant Kidd. The men, all colliers, were later named as William Kearsley, (alias Winstanley), David Millington, Ralph Birchall, James Winstanley, and Richard Pritchard. Kearsley was very well known to the police, having been previously convicted of thefts from railway wagons and having undergone a long prison sentence for a violent assault. Kearsley, Pritchard and Millington were taken to the Wigan infirmary, where DC Osborne confronted them. Osborne immediately identified Kearsley as one of his assailants.

A detailed search was also made of the railway sidings and the crime scene. Within the sidings it was found that some of the wagons had been interfered with, and ropes securing tarpaulin sheets to the wagons had been cut. There was also evidence of recent pilfering having taken place from one wagon where a carton containing sweets had been cut open, and some of the contents removed. A jar of sweets which had already been removed was found on the ground close to the wagon. Two other wagons had been rifled, but it was not thought that any of the contents had been stolen. Some men's caps were also found lying on the ground at the crime scene close to where DS Kidd had been stabbed. They were retained by police.

Shortly before noon that morning, the five prisoners were taken before magistrates at the Wigan Borough Police Court, charged with being concerned in the wilful murder of Sergeant Kidd. The prisoners who were all described by the press at the time as rough-looking, did not seem to recognise the severity of their position. The court itself was packed with people, and many others were congregating outside, having been unable to gain admission.

Superintendent Macintosh briefly outlined the circumstances of the case, and asked for a remand in custody, due to the serious nature of the crime, and the probability of further arrests. He stated that the prisoners had been arrested between half past two and seven o'clock that morning. He went on to say that the murdered man was repeatedly stabbed in the neck and face, and his body lay at the railway station temporary mortuary, pending the coroner's inquiry. Asked if they had any objection to a remand in custody, the prisoners replied in the negative. Kearsley, however, declared that he knew nothing about the affair, and Winstanley expressed the intention of providing an alibi. The prisoners were remanded in custody until Thursday, 3 October.

Enquiries continued throughout the day, and they began to focus on two public houses, both within the vicinity of the railway sidings. Enquiries at the New Inn revealed that some of suspects were drinking in the establishment from about six o'clock on the evening of the murder. They left the pub at about a quarter past seven to visit the railway sidings. Later, the same men visited another pub, the Fox Tavern, where they continued drinking together.

The following day, a sixth man, William Halliwell, was also arrested in connection with the incident. Attempts had been made by police to locate Halliwell the previous evening, as he was one of the main suspects in the murder of Sergeant Kidd. However, he did not return home that night, and it later transpired that he had spent the night sleeping rough on a boat which was berthed on the canal. Halliwell was subsequently identified by DC Osborne as the man who had grabbed his truncheon, and he bore traces of the encounter in the form of marks and bruising on his forehead and legs, consistent with having been struck with the truncheon by Osborne. William Halliwell was also remanded in custody.

The following day two more men were arrested and charged in connection with the murder. They were named as Elijah Winstanley and James Williams (alias Wellens), and they too were remanded in custody. A total of eight prisoners were now in custody, being held on suspicion of being involved in the murder.

An inquest into the death of Detective Sergeant Robert Kidd, aged 37, of 17 Zebra Street, Salford was carried out by Mr H. Milligan, Deputy Coroner for the Borough of Wigan. Evidence was presented by local medical practitioner Dr C.R. Graham, who carried out the postmortem. He had been assisted by Dr Roocroft, a police surgeon from Wigan, who corroborated his findings. It was stated that a total of nine stab wounds were found on the victim's head, face and right side of the neck, and death was due to syncope and loss of blood from the severe stab wounds on his neck. Several other witnesses also gave evidence at the inquest.

After extensive police enquires, five of the prisoners were released from custody without charge: David Millington, Ralph Birchall, James Winstanley, Richard Pritchard and James Williams.

The remaining three prisoners – Elijah Winstanley, William Kearsley and William Halliwell – were each charged with the wilful murder of DS Robert Kidd and remanded in custody to appear before Wigan Magistrates on Thursday 10 October 1895.

On Thursday,10 October the three prisoners were taken before the Wigan Magistrates. The court was packed, and hundreds of people were unable to gain admission. Great excitement manifested itself in consequence of the probability of the full facts of the case being disclosed.

Mr Kershaw, who appeared for the prosecution said that since he had been instructed, he had given careful consideration to all the available evidence and agreed with the railway officials that they should not prefer the charge of murder against Halliwell. He asked therefore that Halliwell might be dismissed on that charge, to be called as a witness to give evidence against the other prisoners. Halliwell would, however, still face a charge of wounding Detective Osborne. The court agreed.

As Mr Kershaw outlined the facts as to what had occurred on the night in question, the defendant Winstanley appeared unwell, and a glass of water was obtained for him. Whilst he was sitting down, a commotion arose in the dock, at which time Winstanley rose to his feet and began struggling desperately with four officers, who had to restrain him to keep him under control. The scuffle lasted for several minutes during which time Winstanley shouted, 'I did it. but they are telling a pack of lies. I didn't mean to do it'. This episode caused great excitement in court, but Winstanley gradually quietened down, and sat as if exhausted between two constables. Mr Kershaw continued and detailed the evidence to be given by Halliwell. He also identified Kearsley and likened him to Winstanley.

Detective Constable Osborne then gave his evidence, after which William Halliwell was called into the witness box. Halliwell admitted struggling with Detective Constable Osborne, and whilst doing so, he saw Detective Sergeant Kidd rush by in pursuit of Winstanley and Kearsley, and he heard him struggling with them nearby. Later that evening Halliwell met Winstanley in the Fox Tavern in Chapel Lane, by prior arrangement, and he asked Winstanley how he had got on with his man. Winstanley said that he did not think that the man he was engaged with would live, because he had stabbed him several times after struggling with him. It was thought that the knife used by Winstanley to stab Sergeant Kidd was not being carried by him to be used as a weapon, but to enable him to cut the ropes which secured tarpaulins to the railway wagons.

The next witness to be called was Elizabeth Kearsley, daughter of William Kearsley, whom the prosecuting solicitor said he called with regret. She gave evidence that after her father came home on Sunday night, she heard him say to her mother, 'Our Elijah (meaning Winstanley) has stabbed a bobby in the face with a knife on the railway.' After some further evidence, Winstanley and Kearsley were committed for trial on the capital charge.

Counsel for the prosecution then stated that, as the prisoners had already been committed on the major charge, he should only offer evidence against Halliwell. Accordingly, Kearsley and Winstanley were removed to the cells, leaving Halliwell alone in the dock. Detective Osborne and the surgeon who attended him were examined, and Halliwell, who reserved his defence, was committed to stand trial at the Liverpool Assizes.

On Tuesday 26 November the case appeared before Justice Henn Collins at the Liverpool Assizes. Elijah Winstanley aged 31 and William Kearsley aged 43 were both charged with the wilful murder of Robert Kidd. William Halliwell aged 31 was charged with feloniously wounding William Henry Osborne. The three defendants pleaded not guilty.

Mr Pickford QC and Mr Kershaw appeared for the crown. Mr McKeand represented Winstanley, Mr Cunningham represented Kearsley and Mr Ambrose-Jones represented Halliwell.

Judge Collins instructed that Halliwell be removed from the dock for him to be called as a witness to give queen's evidence against Winstanley and Kearsley in the principal trial of wilful murder.

Evidence was given by the prosecution witnesses, including Halliwell, who under oath gave a detailed account of the incident including the admission made by Winstanley in the Fox Tavern regarding the stabbing of Kidd and his admission that he did not think the man would live. Whilst giving his evidence, Halliwell fainted and had to be carried from the witness box. Another witness was called until Halliwell had recovered sufficiently to resume and finish giving his evidence.

After presentation of the case for the prosecution, the defence failed to call any witnesses which included Kearsley and Winstanley, but the defence counsel representing Kearsley insisted that he was not involved in the fatal attack in any way and urged the jury to acquit him. Counsel acting on behalf of Winstanley asked the jury not to credit Halliwell's story.

His Lordship in his summing up of the evidence, showed in what particulars Halliwell's story was corroborated.

Upon conclusion of the trial, the jury deliberated for a mere ten minutes and without leaving the courtroom they returned a verdict of guilty against Winstanley and Kearsley on the capital charge of wilful murder.

Winstanley and Kearsley were both sentenced to death.

On the direction of the Judge, no evidence was offered against William Halliwell who had given queen's evidence at the trial. He was discharged.

After the two men had been found guilty of the wilful murder of Robert Kidd, the accused Elijah Winstanley declared that he himself had stabbed Kidd to death, and that Kearsley did not take any active part in it.

It was later decided that the death sentence imposed upon William Kearsley be commuted to life imprisonment. A letter was later sent from the Home Secretary to Mr James Wilson, the solicitor acting for Mr Kearsley, stipulating that the sentence imposed upon his client would be further considered after the prisoner had completed a minimum of ten years penal servitude, although no pledge could be given of the result which may then be arrived at.

William Kearsley served his penal servitude at Dartmoor Prison. He did not serve the minimum ten years as instructed by the Home Secretary. He was released from Dartmoor in February 1903 after serving seven years and three months. Upon his release, he returned home to his family in Wigan.

Elijah Winstanley was hanged at Walton Prison, Liverpool, on 17 December 1895. His body was later buried within the precincts of the prison. The person who carried out the execution was Mr James Billington from Bolton in Lancashire.

Thomas Scott from Huddersfield had been designated as the assistant executioner and had reported to the prison the previous evening. Scott then decided to have a 'night on the town', and later that evening he picked up a local prostitute, 29-year-old Winifred Webb with whom he had sex. A short time later he discovered that she had stolen his wallet, so he reported the matter to the local police. Webb was later arrested and found to be in possession of a wallet and a pair of spectacles belonging to Mr Scott. When the police found out that Scott was due to officiate at the execution of Winstanley, they contacted the Home Office, and he was immediately relieved of his duties. He never again performed duty as an assistant executioner in England and Wales, although he did continue to perform his duties in Ireland where he was the chief executioner and continued to do so until 1901. James Billington conducted the execution of Winstanley without an assistant being present.

The victim in this tragic case was Detective Sergeant Robert Kidd, aged 37. He had originally served as a constable in the Manchester City Police Force, before leaving to join the LNWR Police in 1885. He performed duties as a uniformed constable before being appointed detective constable at Warrington in 1887. He transferred to Liverpool (Edge Hill Station) the following year and was promoted to detective sergeant at Manchester in 1889. He remained in that post until his death. At the time of his death, he was living at 17 Zebra Street, Salford with his wife Ellen and their seven children, all under the age of twelve.

Whilst numerous officers in the employ of the various railway police forces have died or been killed whilst on duty, most of these deaths were caused by accidents, sudden illness or casualties of war. Fortunately, only a handful of officers have died because of acts of violence towards them whilst carrying out their duties. This however can occur when an officer happens to be in the wrong place at the wrong time. One such officer was Detective Sergeant Robert Kidd, who should be remembered for his courage, bravery, and of course his devotion to duty, for which he paid the ultimate price.

On 29 September 2021, the 126th anniversary of the murder of Detective Sergeant Robert Kidd, a blue plaque was unveiled at Wigan North Western Railway Station, by Superintendent Alderson of the British Transport Police in commemoration of Sergeant Kidd, on behalf of the British Transport

Police History Group. The event was attended by serving and retired police officers, railway staff and descendants of Sergeant Kidd's family.

Body found in Train Compartment

Elizabeth Annie Camp, aged 33, lived at the Good Intent public house in East Street, Walworth, South London, where she worked as a barmaid. She was an attractive woman and very popular with the customers who visited the pub. Elizabeth was a single woman, but engaged to be married to a greengrocer, Edward Berry who also lived in Walworth.

On Thursday 11 February 1897, Elizabeth spent the day with her sister, after visiting her house in Hounslow, West London. She left to return home at about 7pm that evening, accompanied by her sister, who walked with her to Hounslow Railway Station in order to catch the 7.42pm train to London Waterloo. Her fiancée Edward had arranged to meet her at Waterloo to escort her back home to Walworth. Elizabeth boarded the train at Hounslow and sat in a second-class compartment. There was no other occupant in the compartment when the train left the station, and her sister waved her goodbye.

After the train departed from Hounslow, it stopped at Isleworth, Putney, Wandsworth, Clapham Junction and Vauxhall stations before arriving at Waterloo Station on time at 8.25pm. Edward Berry was at Waterloo station standing on the station concourse just outside the ticket barrier when the train arrived, but as all the passengers alighted from the train there was no sign of Elizabeth. He decided to remain at the station to see if she would be on the next train. Not long afterwards, Edward noticed some people congregating on the station platform alongside the train which was still standing at the platform. He walked along the platform to see what was going on and was informed that the body of a woman had been found on the train.

A short time earlier, after all the passengers had alighted from the train, some carriage cleaners began sweeping out the compartments and picking up litter when suddenly, one of the cleaners made a shocking discovery. Lying on the floor in a second-class compartment, with her head wedged beneath a seat was the body of Elizabeth Camp. It appeared that she had been beaten to death by heavy blows to the head, smashing her skull from which brain parts were protruding. Although the body was still warm, she was obviously dead with blood all over the compartment floor. The alarm was raised and officers of the London and South Western Railway Police, stationed at Waterloo arrived within minutes and a murder investigation was launched. The investigation was conducted jointly by Superintendent Robinson (LSWR Police) and Detective Inspector Marshall (Scotland Yard, Metropolitan Police).

Elizabeth Camp's body was removed to St Thomas's Hospital where she was certified as being dead on arrival and it was formally identified by the grief-stricken fiancée of Miss Camp, Edward Berry. Enquiries later revealed that a violent struggle had taken place in the train compartment, during which the victim had been struck numerous times to the head with a blunt instrument, shattering her skull. Inside the compartment where the murder had taken place, were the remains of a broken umbrella which had belonged to Miss Camp. Seat cushions were heavily bloodstained and large quantities of blood were spread over the floor of the compartment. A postmortem examination of the body showed that there were no signs indicating that any sexual assault had taken place and investigating officers reached the conclusion that robbery was deemed to have been the most likely motive for the murder. Prior to Miss Camp boarding the train, she went with her sister to the station booking office and purchased a second-class ticket to Waterloo. She paid for the ticket with money that she was carrying in a green purse. Neither the purse nor the ticket was found on the body of the victim, or in the train compartment in which she had travelled. They were never recovered.

After several adjournments, an inquest into the death of Elizabeth Camp was finally concluded on 7 April 1897 when the coroner's jury returned a verdict that Elizabeth Annie Camp was wilfully murdered by some person or persons unknown.

Extensive police enquiries continued into the murder of Elizabeth Camp over a long period of time and several possible suspects were interviewed by police. Unfortunately, the enquiries carried out were to no avail, and the crime remained unsolved.

Child's Body Found in a Station Toilet

Louise Masset was born and raised in France. She had a French father and an English mother. In 1892, at the age of 32, whilst still unmarried, she gave birth to a son who was christened Manfred Masset. The child's father was a wealthy Frenchman. Due to the stigma attached to illegitimate births in those days, Louise decided to move to London and went to live with her married sister in Bethune Road, Stoke Newington. She kept in touch with Manfred's father who provided for his son by sending money to Louise on a regular basis. Louise obtained employment in London as a daytime governess for a wealthy family.

When Manfred attained the age of three, his mother placed him in the care of a Miss Gentle who raised the boy at her home in Tottenham, London. Louise visited her son regularly, and paid Miss Gentle for his keep. In October 1899, Louise told Miss Gentle that the father of the boy was taking custody of him so that he could raise and educate their son in France. Arrangements were later made for Miss Gentle to take Manfred to London Bridge Railway Station to be handed over to Louise. These arrangements were later altered, and Miss Gentle was told to hand over the boy to Louise outside a public house at Stamford Hill. At about 12.45pm on 27 October, Manfred was handed over to his mother by Miss Gentle as arranged.

After collecting the child, Louise and the boy travelled by bus from Stamford Hill to London Bridge Railway Station, arriving at about 1.45pm that afternoon. They entered the station and went into a waiting room, where Louise informed the attendant that she had arranged to meet someone there. Louise and the boy remained in the waiting room until approximately 2.45pm when they left. Louise informed the waiting room attendant that they were going to the refreshment room. The attendant did not see the boy again, but she did see Louise alone, washing her hands in the ladies' toilet just after 7pm that evening.

Just half an hour earlier the naked body of Manfred Masset had been found, wrapped in a black shawl, in a ladies' toilet attached to the waiting room of Dalston Junction Railway Station in East London. Examination of the body showed that death had been caused by suffocation, but a serious injury had been inflicted by blows with a heavy object to the head, just before, or immediately after death. Lying beside the body was a clinker brick, almost identical to the bricks used in a rock garden at the home of Louise Masset in Stoke Newington. It later transpired that Louise Masset did not go home that evening but caught the 7.22pm train from London Bridge to Brighton instead. During subsequent enquiries, it was established that Louise had purchased a black shawl from a shop in Stoke Newington just three days prior to the murder. The shawl which she purchased was identical to the one wrapped around the body of her child when it was discovered at Dalston Junction Railway Station.

The following afternoon, a brown paper parcel was found in the waiting room at Brighton Railway Station. Examination of the parcel found that it contained the clothing of a child, from which labels and trimmings had been removed, presumably to prevent identification. The clothing was later shown to Miss Gentle, who by means of a particular tear, and a grease mark, was able to identify the clothes as those worn by Manfred Masset on the day his body was found.

Miss Gentle also identified the body found at Dalston Junction Station as being that of Manfred Masset.

On the morning of Monday, 30 October, police visited the home of Louise Masset in Stoke Newington, only to find that she had left the house earlier that morning and gone to Brighton. In a statement later, she said that she had read of the murder of her son in a newspaper, and in a panic had gone to visit her brother-in-law in Brighton, to whom she said, 'I am wanted for murder, but I have not done it.' She was advised by her brother-in-law to go to the police but was afraid to do so. On Wednesday, 1 November, Louise Masset was arrested by police in Croydon.

After her arrest, she protested her innocence. She agreed to take part in an identification parade and was picked out by the waiting room attendant employed at London Bridge Station who saw her leave the waiting room with the boy on the afternoon in question, and return alone shortly after seven o'clock, just half an hour after the body of Manfred had been discovered. Louise told the police that she went to London Bridge Station to hand over the boy to two women who had offered to take care of him for an annual payment of twelve pounds. She was unable to identify either of the two women. She was later charged with the wilful murder of her son Manfred at Dalston Police Station. In reply to the charge she said, 'Impossible.'

A coroner's inquest was held at Hackney on Thursday 16 November 1899, where a jury returned a verdict of wilful murder of Manfred against his mother Louise Masset. She was committed to stand trial at the Central Criminal Court, London, on a Coroner's Warrant.

The trial took place at the Old Bailey on Monday, 18 December. Mr Justice Bruce presided. Lord Coleridge represented the defendant who pleaded not guilty to a charge of wilful murder.

After the prosecution case was presented, Lord Coleridge emphasised that no witnesses had seen Louise Masset at Dalston Junction railway station on the day of the murder and suggested that it was possible that one of the two women described but not named by Masset had committed the crime, and then gone to Brighton, knowing that the prisoner was going there. That person could then have left the parcel of clothing at the station to incriminate the mother of the child. The jury however did not accept this version of events, and after deliberating for just twenty-five minutes found Masset guilty of the wilful murder of her son. She was sentenced to death by hanging. After the verdict was announced, Judge Bruce asked Masset if she had anything to say. She continued to protest her innocence. Throughout the trial, Louise Masset had exhibited the upmost composure, but when the judge assumed the black cap, she broke down, and at the conclusion of the proceedings was in such a state of collapse that she had to be assisted from the dock by two female wardens.

After her conviction was made public, Louise continued to protest her innocence, and a petition on her behalf was organised by the French governesses and residents in London which was sent to Queen Victoria, but the law took its course, and sentence was carried out. Louise did however confess to the murder of her son, just before she was hanged at Newgate prison on Tuesday, 9 January 1900.

Chapter 4

Early Twentieth Century

Shots Fired in a Railway Carriage

On Thursday, 17 January 1901, Rhoda King, a married woman aged 54, who lived in Southampton, caught the 11.20am London and South-Western Railway train from Southampton to London Waterloo, to visit a sick relative. She sat in the corner of an empty third-class carriage with her back to the engine.

A short while later, the train stopped at Eastleigh and George Henry Parker, aged 23, a former soldier, entered the carriage and sat in the other corner seat to Mrs King, also with his back to the engine. He was travelling to Birmingham (via London) to visit his father.

The train continued towards London before stopping at Winchester where William Pearson, a wealthy middle-aged farmer boarded the train. Pearson entered the same compartment as Parker and King and sat directly opposite Parker, facing the engine. Pearson began reading a newspaper but eventually he fell asleep.

None of the three persons in the carriage spoke to each other but as the train approached Surbiton, Parker got up from his seat and went to the toilet. He remained inside the toilet whilst the train was stationary at Surbiton Station. It was later established that during the time Parker was in the toilet, he was loading a revolver which he was carrying in his inside pocket.

When the train left Surbiton, Parker came out of the toilet and sat back down in his seat. As the train neared London, it passed through Vauxhall on its approach to Waterloo Station, so Mrs King stood up from her seat and looked out of the carriage window whilst getting her train ticket out of her purse. Suddenly she heard two loud bangs. Although startled, she thought they were fog warning detonators, until she turned around and saw that Parker, who was holding a revolver, had shot Pearson who was slumped in the corner of his seat. Mrs King then felt blood running down her cheek and realised that she too had been shot just above her jaw.

She immediately turned to Parker and said, 'My god, what have you done?' Parker replied, 'I did it to get some money, I want some money'. King told him she only had one shilling in her purse (£12 today), which Parker took from her. Mrs King was by this time bleeding profusely from her cheek, which necessitated her pressing two handkerchiefs to her face to try to stem the flow of blood.

Parker then leaned over Pearson who was still slumped in the corner of the carriage, apparently dead, having been shot through the head. Parker rifled through his pockets, removing a cigar case and a purse containing a considerable amount of cash which included some gold sovereigns. Parker offered one of the sovereigns to Mrs King in return for her silence, but she refused. Mrs King begged Parker to spare her life and not to shoot her again. Parker then apologised to Mrs King, saying that he was sorry for shooting her.

Still afraid that Parker may use the gun on her again, Mrs King suggested that he should get rid of it, and she was relieved when he took her advice and threw it out of the train widow just as the train was pulling into Waterloo station.

As the train came to a halt, Parker jumped from the carriage and hurried towards the ticket barrier, followed by Mrs King who was in hot pursuit. Even though she was on the point of collapse, she managed to tell two railwaymen to chase Parker as he had just killed somcone. She then collapsed before being conveyed to St Thomas' Hospital for treatment for her injuries. She was unconscious upon arrival and remained in hospital for over a week before she was well enough to be discharged. She bore a facial scar, left by the bullet wound, for the rest of her life.

Meanwhile, following the shooting incident, Parker was pursued by railway staff as he ran out of Waterloo Station. He entered the premises of the Metropolitan Gasworks where they eventually found him hiding in an alcove.

Police were quickly on the scene and Parker was swiftly arrested. He told the officers, 'I should have killed the woman as well, then I could have got away with it.' He was taken into police custody, and a murder enquiry was conducted jointly by Superintendent Robinson and Detective Inspector Scott of the South-Western Railway police and Detective Inspector Allen and Detective Sergeant Thorley of the Metropolitan police.

The cigar case, together with the purse and contents belonging to Pearson, were still in the possession of Parker when he was arrested. The revolver used in the shooting was later recovered by police from the railway track just outside Waterloo Station. It was later established that the revolver had been loaded with six bullets, two of which had been discharged, one into Pearson and the other into Mrs King.

A postmortem was later carried out on William Pearson, who had been killed by a single shot through the head.

George Parker subsequently appeared before Westminster Magistrates Court where he was indicted to stand trial at the Old Bailey in London for the wilful murder of William Pearson and the attempted murder of Rhoda King. He was remanded in custody.

On Friday, 1 March, George Henry Parker, alias George Henry Hill, appeared before Mr Justice Phillimore at the Central Criminal Court in London charged with the wilful murder of William Pearson and the unlawful wounding of Rhoda King with intent to murder her.

Mr A. Gill conducted the prosecution and Mr Percival Clarke represented the defendant. A plea of not guilty was entered on both counts.

Overwhelming evidence was presented before the court and the jury found Parker guilty on both counts. The court also heard that Parker had served as a soldier in the army but had been discharged for misconduct after being found guilty of larceny. He was a petty criminal, a heavy drinker and was frequently found in a drunken state.

After the conclusion of the trial, Mr Justice Phillimore donned his black cap before passing the death sentence on Parker. He was remanded to Wandsworth Prison where he was detained pending his execution of death by hanging.

Whist incarcerated, he wrote a letter to Mrs Pearson, wife of his murder victim, showing remorse for his crimes and begging her forgiveness for the murder of her husband. It is not known if Mrs Pearson ever replied to the letter.

At 6am on Tuesday, 26 March, the Reverend Mr J. Phipps, a prison chaplain, visited the condemned cell inside Wandsworth Prison, together with two prison officers. The prisoner who had slept very little during the night, ate breakfast sparingly before the last rites and Christian devotions were administered.

Shortly before 9am Parker was escorted from his cell to the prison courtyard where his execution was to take place. He walked with a firm step to the scaffold, where at 9am precisely, in the presence of the Reverend Phipps, Major Knox and the Prison Governor, Mr Billington carried out the execution, with his son acting as his assistant. Three prison officers were also standing by. Billington later confirmed that the execution had gone without a hitch and that death was instantaneous.

A large crowd of people had gathered outside the prison to watch the hoisting of the black flag after the execution had taken place. The body of Parker was later interred within the precinct of the prison.

Murder of a Railway Detective

Sometime after 6pm, on Saturday, 10 August 1901, a young Railway Detective Constable by the name of Thomas Hibbs, aged just 23, of the LNWR Police, was on duty patrolling Curzon Street railway goods sidings in Birmingham. He was checking some coal wagons stabled there, following complaints from local coal merchants that coal was being stolen from the wagons.

What happened next is subject to some conjecture, but it is thought that whilst patrolling the sidings, he saw three men stealing coal from one of the wagons. The men each filled a sack with coal, placed the sacks over their shoulders and left the sidings. Detective Hibbs followed the men from the sidings and along Fazeley Street leading towards the Birmingham Canal where he shouted at the men to stop. Two of the men dropped their sacks of coal (later recovered by police) and fled the scene. The third man also ran away but continued to carry his sack of coal on his shoulder. Hibbs gave chase as they ran along the Birmingham Canal towpath to the junction of the Birmingham and Warwick Canal where he caught up with them.

The man carrying the sack of coal threw it into the canal, after which the three men turned on Hibbs.

Hibbs drew out his truncheon to defend himself but was overwhelmed and forced onto the floor. It is thought that one of the men grabbed hold of the police truncheon and after wrenching it from his hand, used it to strike him on the back of his head, causing a severe fracture to the skull which was later discovered during a postmortem examination of the body. Although still alive, but possibly unconscious, Hibbs was then thrown into the canal where he later drowned. It was presumed that Hibbs had been finished off to prevent him from identifying his assailants.

Shortly after 8.30pm that evening, James Lea, a local vagrant, was walking alongside the canal when he discovered the body of Thomas Hibbs lying in the water, so he sounded the alarm. Officers from the Birmingham City Police were quickly on the scene, followed by officers of the LNWR Police. A joint murder enquiry was immediately launched by both police forces.

The body of Detective Hibbs was later retrieved from the canal, and the following morning police dragged the canal in the area where the body had been found. There, they recovered the sack of coal stolen from the railway, together with a police truncheon and a pair of police handcuffs which had belonged to Hibbs.

Acting on information received, police subsequently arrested three men in connection with the murder. The men were later named as Frank Parslow, aged 24, William Billingsley, aged 23 and Charles Webb, aged 21.

William Billingsley was interviewed by Detective Inspector Moxon and made a written statement in which he admitted stealing coal from Curzon Street railway sidings, along with Parslow and Webb on the evening in question. He further admitted that they were confronted by Detective Hibbs on the canal towpath. Billingsley went on to say that Hibbs attempted to handcuff Parslow and Webb and a struggle took place between the three of them, but he took no active part in it. He did however deny that anyone struck Hibbs on the head with his police truncheon. He went on to say that following the struggle, Hibbs who was very much alive, was left lying on the canal towpath as the three of them ran away. He strongly denied that Hibbs had been thrown into the canal.

When Parslow and Webb were interviewed, they refused to comment about the events of that evening, but they strongly denied striking Hibbs on the head or throwing him into the canal.

On Thursday, 29 August, a full coroner's inquest into the death of Thomas Hibbs was held before the Birmingham Coroner Isaac Bradley. During the hearing, both Frank Parslow and Charles Webb continued to deny any involvement in assaulting Hibbs or throwing him into the canal.

The written statement made by William Billingsley in the presence of DI Moxon was read out at the hearing, but the contents were retracted by Billingsley who told the inquest that although he made the statement, he only did it for a bit of fun and there was no truth in it.

Another witness, Albert McCulloch, brother-in-law of Frank Parslow, gave evidence of an alleged conversation which took place between Frank Parslow and his father at their home, in which Frank implicated himself and Charles Webb as being involved in the murder of Hibbs. Parslow denied that any such conversation took place. Other family members gave evidence that they were in the house at the time, and they also declared that no such conversation ever took place and that nothing of the kind was said.

In his summing up, Coroner Bradley pointed out that all the evidence presented was circumstantial, there were no independent witnesses to the murder and that there had been nothing stated which could enable the jury to properly charge anyone with the crime.

The jury subsequently found that Hibbs was murdered by some person or persons unknown and acting on the suggestion of the coroner, the jury recommended that in future, the railway companies concerned use two detectives instead of one for similar patrols to the one which the deceased was engaged in.

Despite the coroner's inquest concluding that here was insufficient evidence to commit the three suspects to stand trial for murder, they remained in custody until Thursday, 5 September, when they appeared before Birmingham Magistrates Court to be indicted for murder. However, despite further extensive enquiries by police, the prosecutor Mr J.E. Hill informed the Stipendiary Magistrate Mr T.M. Collymore that further anticipated evidence in this case had not been forthcoming and the evidence available to secure a conviction against any of the three prisoners was so flimsy that he felt that he must ask the magistrate the let the defendants go. The case of wilful murder against the three defendants was then dismissed by the Stipendiary due to lack of evidence and after informing the men that they could be re-arrested if further evidence came to light, the prisoners were released and left the dock without saying a word.

It should be remembered that in 1901, forensic evidence which we take for granted today, was very much in its infancy and extremely basic. DNA profiling had not been discovered and evidence from eyewitnesses was usually the only way to secure such a conviction. Sadly, there were no witnesses to the event, and the case remains unsolved. Thomas Hibbs had a wife and two young daughters.

Coincidentally, the year 1901, when this offence occurred, was an important milestone in the history of forensic science, as it was the year when fingerprint evidence was first introduced in British Court of law.

Woman's Body found in a Railway Tunnel

At about 11pm on Sunday, 24 September 1905, William Peacock a railway works inspector for the LBSCR, was walking through a mile long railway tunnel located at Merstham, between Croydon and Redhill in Surrey. He was inspecting the interior of the tunnel, following maintenance work which had been carried out on the tunnel earlier that day.

As he made his way through the darkness, the light from his oil lamp shone on what appeared to be a bundle of rags on the ground. As he bent down to pick up the bundle, he made a gruesome discovery. The bundle of rags was in fact the body of a young woman. Her skull had been badly smashed, leaving parts of her brain protruding. Her left leg was almost completely severed from the rest of her body, presumably by the wheels of a train. The body was still warm, indicating that it had not been in the tunnel for any great length of time.

William Peacock presumed that the woman had either been pushed, thrown or jumped from a moving train, so he left the tunnel to raise the alarm. William telephoned the Station Master at Merstham Station who in turn contacted the police and reported the matter. Due to the dangerous location of the body, the local police requested that railway staff recover the body from the tunnel and take it the nearby Feathers Hotel in Merstham, which they did. The body was handed over to police at the hotel. Police initially assumed that the woman's death was as a direct result of her falling out of a moving train, either by accident or suicide. Later, however, a closer inspection of the body revealed that a silk scarf had been forced into the woman's mouth and down her throat. There were also numerous bruises and scratches to her body, consistent with her being in some sort of struggle. It appeared likely that police were no longer investigating an accident or suicide, but something far more sinister. The preliminary evidence suggested that the police were now looking at a murder victim. Nothing was found on the body or inside the tunnel to indicate who the victim was, so the local police circulated details of the incident, along with a description of the victim to the Metropolitan Police and other police forces in the surrounding areas.

On the Tuesday, just two days after the body had been found, Robert Henry Money, a dairy farmer, went into the Metropolitan Police Station at Clapham in South-West London to report that his 22-year-old sister had been missing since leaving work at about 7pm the previous Sunday. The description given matched the body of the victim found inside Merstham tunnel. Later that day, Robert Money formally identified the body as that of his sister, Mary Sophia Money of 245 Lavender Hill, Clapham.

Mary was an attractive and bubbly young lady who was employed as a bookkeeper for Mr Bridger, a dairy farmer in Clapham. She lived at Lavender Hill, London in shared accommodation with a close friend and work colleague Emma Hone. She was a polite, well-mannered individual, well-liked by her friends, neighbours, and work colleagues alike.

On the afternoon of her death, she had been working. Her works colleagues remarked that she seemed to be in a very cheerful mood and seemed excited. At one point that afternoon, she was seen to be furtively studying a railway timetable as if planning a train journey. After finishing work at 7pm she told her friend Emma that she was going for a walk and left the premises, heading in the direction of Clapham Junction Railway Station. Miss Golding, who owned a sweet shop just outside the station, later gave a statement to police, stating that at about 7.20pm, Mary, a regular customer, called into her shop to buy some chocolate, stating that she was on her way to the station to catch a train to Victoria Station in London. That was the last positive sighting of Mary until her body was discovered.

Witnesses also told police that when Mary left work, she was smartly dressed, wearing a black dress, a silk scarf and carrying her knitted purse. It later transpired that the silk scarf she was wearing when she left work was identical to the one which had later been stuffed down her throat shortly before her death. Police were satisfied that it was the same scarf that she had been wearing earlier. Her purse, however, was never found.

Police enquiries later led them to focus their attention on a train which left London Bridge Station at 9.33pm that evening, destined for Brighton. A railway signalman who was working in East-Croydon signal box stated that as the train was passing his signal box, about 8 miles (13km) from Merstham tunnel, he saw a couple standing up in a fist-class compartment near the middle of the train. The man seemed to have grabbed hold of the woman, and they appeared to be quarrelling. He did not give it much thought until he heard about the body being found in the tunnel.

In corroboration of his story, the signalman on duty at Purley Oaks signal box, just 5 miles (8km) from the tunnel also said that a man and a woman were standing up and seemed to be having an altercation in a first-class compartment of the same train. He just dismissed it as a lover's tiff. The train guard was interviewed, and he told police that when the train stopped at Croydon, he saw a female passenger fitting the description of Mary sitting in a first-class compartment in the middle of the train. She seemed to be in the company of a young man.

Other witnesses also reported numerous possible sightings of Mary at both Victoria and London Bridge Stations. Some stated she was alone, others said she was with a man. Some witnesses said the man she was with had ginger hair and was wearing a bowler hat. Nobody matching that description was ever traced.

The 'Brighton Line', as it is commonly known, runs between London and Brighton. The railway line was originally constructed with two London terminus stations, namely Victoria and London Bridge. The line out of both stations heads south towards Brighton until they merge at East Croydon into one line which then continues to Brighton. An extension was later added from London Bridge Station, northwards over a bridge, crossing the river Thames into Charing Cross Station which was built to allow passengers closer access to central London.

Police investigating this case seem to have given more weight to the theory that Mary Money travelled on a London Bridge to Brighton train before meeting her untimely death. This is largely because two separate railway signalmen witnessed what appeared to be a scuffle taking place on the 9.33pm train from London Bridge to Brighton. Altercations and even physical assaults are not uncommon between men and women travelling on trains, yet very few results in serious injury or the death of an individual. The fracas which apparently took place on the 9.33pm train from London Bridge only came to light because a body was found in the tunnel. Whether Mary Money was the woman involved in the dispute on the train, will never be known.

On the other hand, it is known that Mary travelled from Clapham Junction to Victoria from where there was a fast and frequent train service to Brighton. She would have arrived at Victoria Station shortly before 8pm, where she could have easily boarded a train directly to Brighton, which most people would have done. It does seem rather pointless, having arrived at Victoria Station, to travel to London Bridge Station, which is not accessible by a direct train service from Victoria, merely to catch a train to Brighton over one and a half hours later.

Having said that, one can only speculate as to what happened after Mary got off her train at Victoria Station that fateful evening. It does seem likely that she had arranged to meet someone and was excited about doing so. She was also very secretive about it, not even confiding in her closest friend and housemate Emma Hone. Whether she boarded a Brighton train at Victoria or London Bridge we will never know and furthermore, we will never know the full details surrounding her death.

The inquest into the death of Mary Sophia Money was held at the Feathers Hotel in Merstham, after which, an open verdict was announced. The coroner remarked, 'Miss Money met her death by severe injuries brought about by a train, but the evidence was insufficient to show whether she jumped, fell, or was thrown from a train.' No charges were ever brought against anyone in connection with the death of Mary Sophia Money.

Although scratches and bruises, consistent with her being in a struggle were found on her body, and the silk scarf which she had been wearing had been stuffed down her throat and her knitted purse was missing, her death was never officially classified as a murder and still remains a complete mystery.

Murder on the 10.27

John Nisbet, aged 44, a married man from Newcastle, was employed as a bookkeeper/wages clerk at Stobswood Colliery near Widdrington, some 23 miles north of Newcastle. On Friday, 18 March 1910, Nisbet travelled in a third-class compartment of the 10.27am, non-corridor train from Newcastle Central Station to Alnmouth where he was due to change trains to get to Widdrington. Nisbet was in possession of a leather briefcase containing a substantial amount of cash which he had withdrawn from a bank earlier that morning to pay the wages of the workers at the colliery.

The train from Newcastle arrived at Alnmouth at 12.06pm and after the passengers had alighted, the station porter Tom Charlton walked along the platform, closing all the doors which had been left open. He eventually came to the compartment where Nisbet had been sitting. The compartment appeared to be empty, but he noticed that a window had been left open, so he decided to close it. Upon opening the compartment door to close the window, porter Charlton saw blood on the floor of the compartment, together with a hat and a pair of broken spectacles. Then, to his horror, he noticed the body of a man lying face down, having been pushed under the seat. The man was in fact, John Nisbet. It transpired that he had been killed by five bullets which had been fired into his head. Charlton immediately reported the matter to the Station Master who summoned the police, and Superintendent Weddell of the Newcastle City Police set-up a murder enquiry.

Enquiries established that on alternate Fridays, John Nisbet would visit Lloyd's Bank in Mosley Street, Newcastle and draw out cash on behalf of his employer, to pay coal miners their fortnightly wages at Stobswood Colliery where he worked. He then travelled to work by catching the 10.27am train from Newcastle to Alnmouth, where he changed trains to continue his journey to Widdrington. He caught the 10.27am train each time he withdrew the wages from the bank.

Further enquiries revealed that on 18 March; he withdrew the sum of £370 9s 6d (£55,000 today) which had been prepared as three canvas bags containing gold sovereigns and several brown paper parcels which contained silver and copper coins. Each of the canvas bags bore the following markings: 'North-Eastern'; 'Lloyd's'; 'No 1 Lambton'. Nisbet placed all the cash into his own leather briefcase before leaving the bank. He was seen to be in possession of the briefcase when he boarded the train at Newcastle, but it was not in the train compartment when the train arrived at Alnmouth. It was apparent therefore that the motive for the murder of John Nisbet was one of robbery.

Charles Raven, a witness in the case, was able to say that he was on Newcastle Station on the day in question when he saw John Nisbet on the station platform in company with John Dickman and they both boarded the train together in the same third-class compartment. Raven had known both men for several years. He knew Nisbet very well and he also knew Dickman, but only by sight, not by name. He was however able to identify him to police as the person who boarded the train with Nisbet.

Mr Hall, another witness who also knew Nisbet, saw him board the train together with another man. He later picked out Dickman from a line of twelve other men in an identity parade. He told police that he was not 100 per cent certain that Dickman was the man with Nisbet, although he was reasonably sure that he was the same person.

William Hepple, another witness, stated that he was at the station that day when he saw John Nisbet, who he knew, boarding the 10.27am train together with another man, matching the description of Dickman. He had never seen the man before, but they both got into the same third-class compartment.

After the train departed Newcastle, the next station stop was Heaton where Nisbet lived. His wife frequently went onto the station platform at Heaton which was near their home and spoke to her husband when he was passing through on his way to work, and she did so on the day in question. Having spoken to her husband through the compartment window, she was able to say that there was just one other person in the compartment when the train left Heaton. It was a man, although she did not think she would be able to recognise him again, because his coat collar was turned up, casting a shadow over his face. Later however, whilst giving evidence in open court at the Magistrates' hearing, she fainted as soon as she saw Dickman and after recovering, she was asked what caused her to faint to which she replied that it was as a result of seeing the defendant in court as he was without doubt the person who was travelling in the same compartment as her husband on the day of the murder. She said that after seeing his profile in court, it all came back to her. Mrs Nisbet later repeated this evidence of identification at Dickman's trial at the Assize Court.

Further enquiries revealed that a person matching the description of Dickman left the train at Morpeth station, the stop before Alnmouth. The witness to this was the station ticket collector, John Athey, who specifically remembered the man because he did not have a train ticket but when stopped, he offered to pay the fare from Stannington which Athey accepted. Athey could not remember whether or not the man was carrying a briefcase. Police searches were carried out in several locations, including some local colliery mineshafts which would have been familiar to Dickman, and the leather briefcase belonging to Nisbet was found abandoned at the bottom of a mine shaft at the Isabella Colliery in Hepscott, just 1½ miles from Morpeth Station where Dickman had alighted from the train. The copper coins which Nisbet had withdrawn from the bank were still in the case, but the gold and silver currency had been removed.

On Monday, 21 March, John Alexander Dickman, a bookmaker and former secretary at Morpeth Colliery, was arrested at his home and taken to Newcastle police station, where he was interviewed by Superintendent Weddell. It was put to him that witnesses had seen him board the 10.27am train to Alnmouth with John Nisbet just three days earlier. Dickman admitted travelling on the train but denied being in company with John Nisbet. He did however admit that he had known Nisbet for about twenty years, having worked with him in the past when he was a ledger clerk in an office at Quayside in Newcastle.

Dickman went on to say that on the day in question he visited Newcastle Central Station to catch a train to Stannington to meet a man called William Hogg who worked at Dovecot Colliery to discuss the sinking of a new colliery mineshaft there. He further stated that he went to the ticket office to buy a ticket, when, just by chance, he saw John Nisbet standing in front of him in the queue. After buying tickets, both men walked towards the platform and boarded the same train. Dickman went on to say that he was walking behind Nisbet and boarded the rear of the train whilst Nisbet walked further along the platform towards the front of the train. Weddell asked him about the witnesses who saw them walk along the platform together before getting into the same compartment, but Dickman said they must have all been mistaken.

When interviewed further, Dickman admitted knowing that Nisbet took the miners' wages to the colliery on alternate Fridays but insisted that it was pure coincidence they happened to catch the same train that day and he still insisted that they had travelled in different compartments, and he was not involved in the murder of Nisbet or stealing the money.

Superintendent Weddell told Dickman that the ticket collector at Morpeth Station remembered him leaving the train there and not at Stannington where he said that he was meeting William Hogg. Dickman replied that during the journey to Stannington, he started reading a newspaper but must have fallen asleep. When he woke up, he realised that the train had already passed Stannington, so he got off at Morpeth, the next stop and paid the excess fare as he left the station.

Dickman was asked what happened next. He stated that he left Morpeth Station with the intention of walking back to Stannington (about four miles), but after walking a short distance, he felt unwell, so he lay down in a field where he fell asleep. When he woke up, he decided to return to Morpeth Station and catch a train back to Newcastle, which he did. He denied walking to the nearby Isabella Colliery and dumping the stolen briefcase down a mineshaft. He was then asked why he did not catch a train back from Morpeth to Stannington straight away, as there was a train due just ten minutes after he arrived there. He said that he didn't know the train times, so he just decided to walk back.

During the investigation, extreme efforts were made to find the revolver used in the shooting, but it was never recovered. However, some less incriminating evidence was found. When Dickman was arrested, police did recover a pair of suede gloves from his home which contained blood stains on both palms, which corresponded with spots of blood which were also found inside both pockets of a pair of trousers recovered from his home. He was unable to account for the stains, either on the gloves or his trousers, stating that he had no idea how they got there. Also recovered from the home of Dickman was an empty canvas cash bag belonging to Lloyds Bank, bearing the words 'No 1 Lambton' which was identical to one of the bags of gold sovereigns handed to Nisbet at Lloyds Bank. When asked about the bag, Dickman was able to show that he himself also had an account with Lloyd's bank. He said he must have got the bag from Lloyds on one of his earlier visits but forgotten to return it.

William Hogg, the man that Dickman said he was going to meet at Stannington on the day of the murder was also seen by police and gave a statement that although he knew Dickman and had met him on three of four occasions recently to discuss the sinking of a mineshaft at Dovecot, he had never arranged to see him on 18 March, either at Dovecot Colliery or anywhere else for that matter, because he was not even working at Dovecot Colliery that day as he was on business in Newcastle.

On Thursday, 14 April Dickman appeared before Newcastle Magistrates Court where he pleaded not guilty to the wilful murder of John Nisbet. He was committed to stand trial at the next session of the Northumberland Assize Court.

On Monday, 4 July John Alexander Dickman appeared before Lord Coleridge at the Northumberland Assizes in Newcastle, charged with the wilful murder of John Nisbet on 18 March 1910. Mr Tindal Atkinson KC conducted the prosecution and Mr Michael Innes KC, assisted by Lord William Percy, represented Dickman who pleaded not guilty.

The trial lasted for two days, after which jury found Dickman guilty of the wilful murder of John Nisbet. After putting on his black cap, Lord Coleridge passed the mandatory sentence of death by hanging upon Dickman, who was then remanded in Newcastle Prison to await his execution.

From the time of his arrest Dickman denied murdering Nisbet. He protested his innocence at the Magistrates' hearing and continued to do so throughout his subsequent trial at the assizes. After sentence was passed, Dickman still protested his innocence. An appeal against conviction was rejected and an appeal for clemency to the Home Secretary, Winston Churchill, was also rejected.

Just before 8am on Tuesday, 9 August, Dickman was escorted from his cell into the courtyard of Newcastle Prison, by the Reverend W.F.

Lumley the Prison Chaplain, Mr Hilliard the Prison Governor and two prison officers. The County Sheriff and his chief clerk were also present. Dickman walked up the gallows steps with Mr Ellis the executioner who carried out the execution, using a 7ft drop. Dickman who never admitted his guilt, did not speak either immediately before or during the execution. It was a clean drop and Dickman died instantly.

John Alexander Dickman was the last person to be hanged at Newcastle Prison. A crowd of over 1,000 spectators, some of whom protested his innocence, assembled outside the prison that day until the hoisting of the black flag and the issuing of the certificate of death, a copy of which was pasted on the prison walls. His body was later interred within the precinct of the prison.

After the execution had been carried out, there was much discussion amongst members of the legal profession and members of the public, about the verdict in this case. The accused always denied any involvement in the murder of John Nisbet. Despite extensive police enquiries, neither the murder weapon nor the stolen cash was ever found.

Forensic science in 1910 was in its infancy compared with today and although blood stains were found on a pair of gloves and trousers belonging Dickman, they could not be linked to Nisbet. The method of determining blood types was not introduced into criminal investigations until 1915, five years after this case.

There were no witnesses to the murder being committed and no witnesses as to the person who disposed of the leather briefcase belonging to the victim down the mine shaft at the Isabella Colliery. All in all, there was no direct evidence to link John Dickman to the murder of John Nisbet. John Dickman therefore became the first ever person in Britain charged with murder to be convicted solely on circumstantial evidence, albeit extremely strong circumstantial evidence.

Stabbed During a Drunken Quarrel

In 1897, Herbert Brooker from Dorking in Surrey left school at the age of 15 to join the Royal Navy. He worked hard and later became a leading seaman. He travelled the world and saw military action in China where he served with distinction before being wounded in action. In 1912, he left the Royal Navy at the age of 30 with a good character reference, and moved into lodgings at Crawley in Sussex, before becoming a lock-gate keeper with the Port of London Authority at the Royal Albert Dock in London.

In December 1913, Brooker met Ada Stone aged 28, whilst she was working as a domestic servant and waitress in a coffee house at Horley in Surrey. She lived on the premises. Although Ada was a married woman, she was separated from her husband who she had not seen for over five years. A relationship between Brooker and Stone quickly developed, and Stone began staying out late in the evenings drinking with Brooker. Her late nights and excessive drinking displeased her employers who gave her several warnings about her bad behaviour.

On Monday, 20 April 1914 Stone arrived back at the coffee house very late in the night, after spending the evening drinking with Brooker. She was drunk and found that she had been locked out of the premises. She started banging on the door and shouting in order to wake the occupants for someone to unlock the door and let her in. She was instantly dismissed from her job for her persistent late nights and drunken behaviour. Stone was told that she must vacate her living quarters and move out of the premises the following day.

Stone spent the rest of that week living with Brooker, and they decided to travel to Brighton that Saturday to spend a few days at the seaside. They started drinking in Horley on the Saturday afternoon and continued drinking until about 8pm, by which time they were both quite drunk. Several people saw them singing on the station platform whilst waiting to catch a train to Brighton. They then boarded the 8.15pm train to Brighton and sat in an empty third-class compartment together. It is not known what happened in that compartment but as the train was approaching Three Bridges Station, a man in the next compartment heard a lot of noise followed by a loud scream. He got up from his seat, leaned out of the window and peered into the next compartment where he saw Stone lying on the compartment floor with Brooker bent over her holding a sheath knife.

The man immediately pulled the communication cord just as the train was pulling into the platform of Three Bridges Station. Brooker quickly jumped from the compartment, slammed the carriage door shut behind him and walked along the station platform towards the station exit. He was still carrying the knife. The man who had witnessed the incident sounded the alarm and Brooker was grabbed by station staff and members of the public before he could leave the station. He put up a violent struggle as he attempted to escape but was restrained. The sheath knife was taken from him, and his arms and legs were tied together. He was then dragged into a nearby waiting room to await the arrival of police.

When the door of the train compartment where the incident occurred was opened, Stone was sitting on the seat and appeared to be sleeping although she was in fact dead. It seemed that Brooker, before alighting from the train, had picked her up from the floor of the compartment and sat her on the seat to allow himself time to get away before anyone noticed the body. It was later established that Ada Stone had been stabbed numerous times in what appeared to be a frenzied attack. One of the stab wounds had severed her pulmonary artery, causing her to bleed to death.

Whilst being restrained in the waiting room pending the arrival of police, Brooker said that he had carried out the attack in a mad frenzy and asked if Stone was dead. Police arrived a short time later and Herbert Brooker was formally arrested and later charged with the wilful murder of Ada Stone.

Brooker was remanded in custody before appearing at the East Grinstead Magistrates Court, where he was committed to the next County Assizes, to stand trial for the wilful murder of Ada Stone. On Tuesday, 7 July, Brooker was brought before Mr Justice Darling at the Sussex Assize Court in Lewes. Eminent barristers Rowland Harker, and Mr St. John Hutchinson appeared for the Crown and Mr F.W. Barrington-Ward represented the accused.

The courtroom was packed with members of the public and those connected with the case, to listen to the trial proceedings which were to last for over five hours. The prisoner, who was smartly dressed in a navy-blue suit, entered the dock, flanked by two prison warders. He pleaded not guilty to the charge of wilful murder of Ada Stone.

Rowland Harker in his opening address to the jury told the court that whilst the prisoner was travelling by train between Horley and Three Bridges on 25 April, in company with his companion Ada Stone, he stabbed and cut her with a knife and inflicted such appalling injuries that when the train arrived at Three Bridges, she was found dead in the carriage. She was a married woman living apart from her husband and had been in domestic service. The prisoner had once served in the Royal Navy and had gained distinction after being wounded in action.

Mr Harker went on to say that by the kindness of the learned counsel representing the prisoner, he had been informed what lines the defence was going to take. He told the jury that the presumption in law is that a man must intend the consequences of his actions. If the defence could prove to the jury that Brooker was in such a state of drunkenness that he was not able to appreciate the difference between right and wrong, and did know what he was doing, then he would be guilty of manslaughter and not murder.

Mr Harker further stated that the jury would have to listen to all the evidence before considering whether Brooker was in such a state of mind to justify a verdict of manslaughter, but he further submitted that after hearing all the evidence, it would be so compelling that it would be their duty to return a guilty verdict on the capital offence of murder.

Mr Barrington-Ward representing the accused submitted that the accused was in such a state of intoxication that he did not realise what he was doing. His only fault throughout life was that he had given way to drink. Counsel suggested to the jury that this was a case of manslaughter, not murder.

The accused gave evidence that he had served in the Royal Navy for fourteen years and left with a good character. He carried a sheath knife concealed down his leg to defend himself, in consequence of an attack made upon him by some men when he was working at the Royal Albert Dock. He was deeply attached to the deceased but did not know she was married when they first met.

Mr Justice Darling in his summing up told the jury that Brooker's defence was that at the time of the murder he was too drunk to have formed any intent to murder. He continued that, although both Brooker and Stone had been drinking heavily that day, there was no evidence to suggest that Brooker showed any such degree of drunkenness to suggest that he did not know what he was doing. On the contrary, his conduct both immediately before and after the murder showed he was in a condition to know perfectly well what he was doing. The moving of Ada Stone's body from the floor to the seat of the carriage and the way he left the train, closing the door behind him before walking quickly along the station platform and his subsequent attempt to escape, were also inconsistent with him being too drunk to be responsible for his actions.

At 5.45pm the jury retired to consider their verdict. They returned after deliberating for just twelve minutes to give a unanimous verdict of guilty against Herbert Brooker for the wilful murder of Ada Stone. The jury did however recommend mercy on account of his previous good character and for the service to his country.

The defendant was then asked if he had anything to say why judgment of death should not be passed upon him. In a low tone he replied, 'Nothing.' The black cap was then placed upon the judge's head and his Lordship addressing the prisoner said that the jury had come to the only possible conclusion upon the evidence presented, that he had wilfully murdered this unfortunate woman with whom he had travelled in the train. The judge then pronounced the mandatory sentence of 'death by hanging' with a recommendation of clemency on account of his previous good character and service in the Royal Navy. The recommendation was later rejected.

On Tuesday, 28 July, Herbert Brooker walked firmly to the scaffold at Lewes Prison in Sussex, where he was hanged by the neck until dead. His body was later buried within the precinct of the prison.

Prior to the execution, in a farewell letter to his landlady at Crawley he wrote, 'Ada was a good girl. I killed her without the slightest reason to my knowledge, for we had no row or anything. The only thing I can think of that caused me to do it was that I must have gone mad'. Brooker then referred to some of his mates and said, 'Keep them off the drink; that is what brought me here'.

The Railway Arch Murder

Miles McHugh, a labourer, aged 30, lived in Chorley, Lancashire, with his wife and two children. After experiencing marital problems, McHugh walked out on his family and moved to Middlesbrough in Yorkshire in the latter part of 1918. Not long afterwards, he met 22-year-old Edith Annie Swainston, to whom he represented himself as a single man. Although Swainston herself was engaged to be married, the couple started seeing each other until a full relationship developed, at which time Edith broke off her engagement with her fiancé.

Although they had a close relationship, McHugh and Swainson did not live together as McHugh preferred to remain living alone in his lodgings. In March 1919, Edith informed McHugh that she was pregnant and later the couple had a child. Edith was still unaware that McHugh was a married man, and their relationship continued until December of that year, when Edith renewed her acquaintance with a man called Holden, her former fiancé.

McHugh subsequently found out that Edith was seeing her former fiancé, and on Christmas Eve, in a jealous rage, he attempted to strangle her, but two other people intervened and prevented him from doing so. On a separate occasion, McHugh confronted Holden, warning him to stay away from Edith as she had borne his child.

In the afternoon of Saturday, 24 January 1920, Edith visited McHugh's lodgings and they went out for a walk together. At about 5pm that day, Margaret Potter saw the couple quarrelling underneath the railway arches leading off Fleetham Street in Middlesbrough. Not long afterwards, a boy walking under one of the arches made a gruesome discovery. The dead body of Edith Swainston was lying on the ground. It was later established that her throat had been cut during a violent struggle which had taken place there. Police were quickly on the scene and a during a search of the crime scene, a blood-stained razor was found.

McHugh was quickly identified as a suspect in the murder of Edith Swainston and was arrested later that night after being found in a drunken stupor. He was bleeding from a nasty cut on a finger of his right hand which was treated at the police station. Initially, he denied knowing a woman by the name of Edith Swainston. Due to his intoxicated state however, it was decided he was too drunk to be interviewed that night, so he remained in a police cell until the following morning.

When interviewed by police the following day, McHugh denied killing Edith Swainston. He was asked how he had cut is finger. Initially he stated that he had cut it on a broken plate, but when questioned further he told officers that he had cut his finger whilst using a penknife.

McHugh later elected to make a statement to the effect that on 24 January, Swainston called at his lodgings. She appeared very low spirited, so they decided to go for a walk. They walked under the railway arches where they started quarrelling, so left her there and started to walk away. He said that he had only walked some three or four yards when he heard a scream. He turned around and saw Swainson draw a razor across her neck, two or three times, cutting her own throat. He dashed towards her and removed the razor from her hand, and in doing so, cut his finger. He said that she slumped to the ground where she died. He went on to say that there was nothing he could do to help her, so he walked way and threw the razor on a nearby waste dump. He further stated that he returned to the scene about an hour later, but when he got there the body was gone. He categorically denied cutting Swainston's throat, insisting that it had been self-inflicted. McHugh was subsequently charged with her murder.

On Tuesday, 9 March, Miles McHugh appeared before the York Assize Court charged with the wilful murder of Edith Swainston on 24 January. He pleaded not guilty. Barristers Mr W.J. Waugh KC and Mr E. Chapman KC prosecuted on behalf of the crown. Mr J.R. MacDonald KC represented the accused. At the conclusion of the trial, it took the jury just twenty minutes to return a guilty verdict against McHugh who was then sentenced to death by hanging. Sentence was carried out at Armley Prison in Leeds on Friday, 16 April.

Murder of a Dedicated Nurse

It was a freezing cold winter's afternoon on Monday, 12 January 1920 when Florence Nightingale Shore, aged 55, arrived at London's Victoria Railway Station to catch a train to Hastings. She was accompanied by an old and trusted friend, Mabel Rogers, who had walked with Florence to the railway station to wave her goodbye.

Shortly after 3pm, the two boarded the 3.20pm passenger train service to Hastings which was standing at the station platform. They sat in an empty third-class compartment where they chatted for a while before Mabel said her goodbyes and alighted from the train. As Mabel left the train, a man entered the same compartment shortly before the train departed. Mabel stood on the station platform and waved goodbye to Florence who was leaning and waving out of the carriage window as the train left the station.

Florence, who was born into a wealthy Derbyshire family, was named after her godmother and second cousin, Florence Nightingale, the famous nurse, often referred to as 'The Lady with The Lamp'. She even followed in her godmother's footsteps, devoting her adult life to nursing the sick. Florence Nightingale Shore even travelled abroad to tend sick and wounded soldiers of the British Armed Forces. She worked in South Africa during the Second Boer War and served both in the Queen Alexandra's Military Nursing Service in England and with the French Red Cross in France, during the First World War. She was held in very high esteem by all who knew her. After the end of the Great War, Florence went to live at the Royal British Nurses' Association nursing home at Hammersmith in North-West London, where her lifelong friend Mabel Rogers was the matron in charge. She remained there until the time of her death.

After departing Victoria Station, the train travelled non-stop for about one hour before stopping at Lewes Station, followed by Polegate some thirty minutes later. The next station stop was Eastbourne where three workmen entered the compartment occupied by Florence Nightingale Shore. She was the only person in the compartment, sitting in a corner seat facing forward, seemingly asleep with what appeared to be a veil covering her face. Some fifteen minutes later, the train arrived at Bexhill and one of the workmen, George Clout, went over to Florence to rouse her. As he got close to her, he realised that her face was not covered by a veil but was in fact covered in blood, emanating from a wound on the top of her head. It was later established that she had received multiple blows to the skull. Florence was conveyed to Hastings hospital in a critical condition, where she died just four days later. She was subsequently buried at the City of Westminster Cemetery in Hanwell, Middlesex (now part of the London Borough of Ealing).

It appeared that the culprit in this case was the unknown man who joined the train at Victoria Station just prior to departure, leaving the train at either Lewes or Polegate, before the workmen joined the train at Eastbourne.

After the attack on Florence was discovered by the workmen and the alarm sounded, the police and ambulance services were quickly on the

Artist's impression of John Tawell on trial at Aylesbury Assizes for the murder of Sarah Hart at Slough in 1845. (P. 12–14).

Franz Muller. Executed in 1864 after he was found guilty of killing Thomas Briggs in the first railway passenger train murder. (P. 28–33).

Percy Mapleton Lefroy. Convicted of murdering and robbing Frederick Gold before throwing him from a moving train during a journey on the Brighton line in 1881. (P. 37–39).

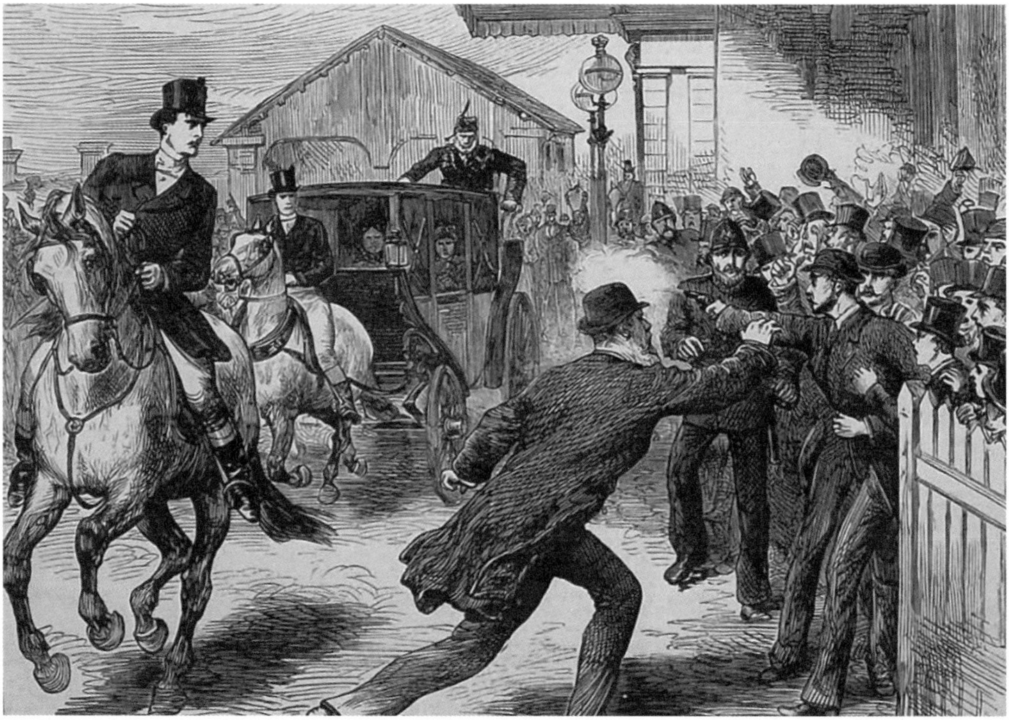

Depiction of the attempted assassination of Queen Victoria at Windsor Railway Station, carried out by Roderick MacLean in 1882. (P. 39–40).

Artist's impression of Samuel Botelier Bristowe, a High Court Judge who was shot whilst boarding a train, during an assassination attempt at Nottingham in 1889. (P. 40-41).

A typical late nineteenth-century London Underground Station targeted by the IRA during the Fenian bombing campaign carried out on mainland Britain during the 1880s. (P. 41–42).

Detective Sergeant Robert Kidd. Stabbed to death whilst attempting to arrest thieves involved in stealing from unattended railway wagons at Wigan in 1895. (P. 49–57).

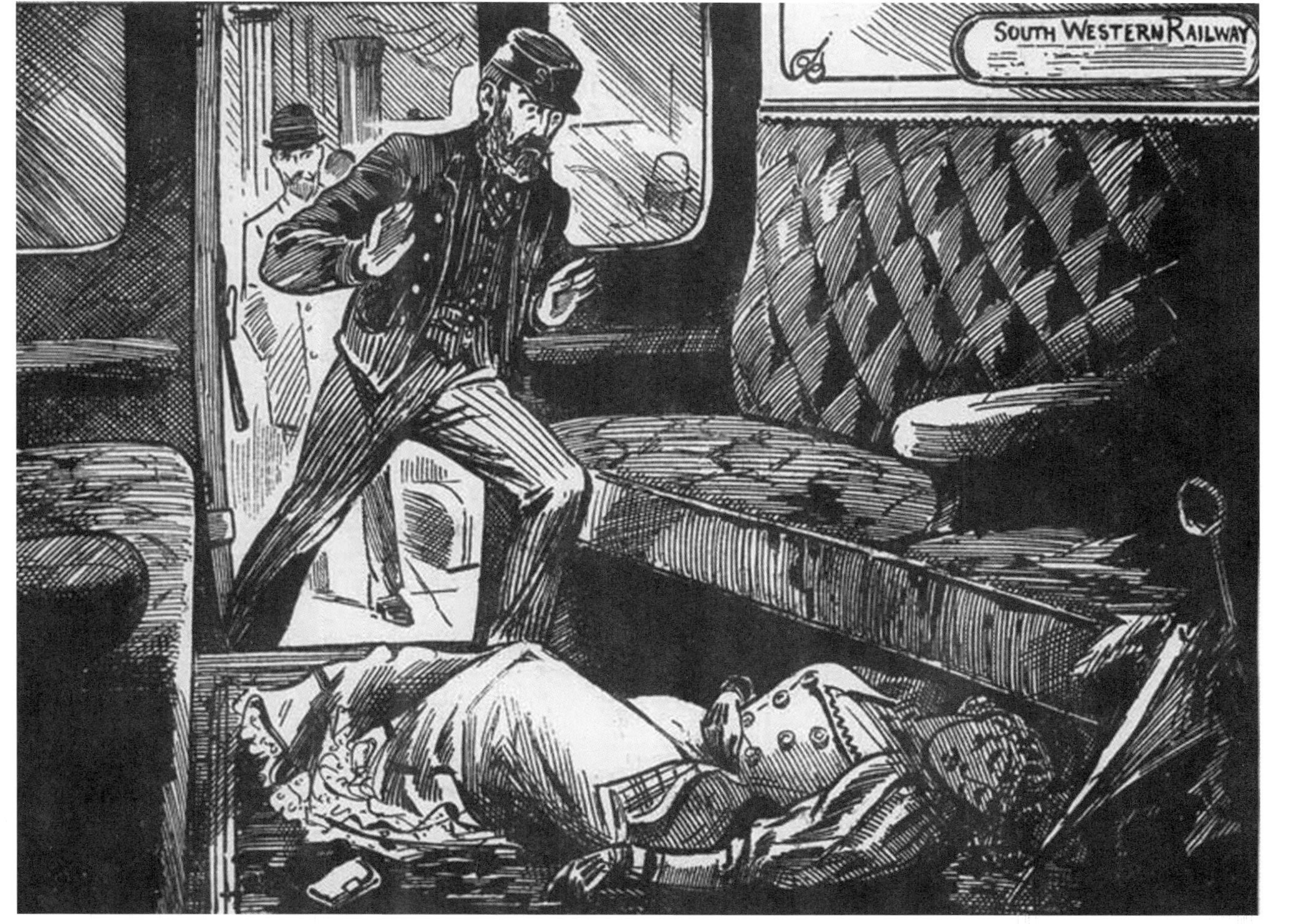

Depiction of the body of Eliabeth Camp, found murdered in a train compartment upon arrival at Waterloo Station, following a 45-minute journey from Hounslow in 1897. (P. 57–58).

Execution of Louise Masset at Newgate Prison in London in 1900. Following her trial at the Old Bailey, she was found guilty of murdering her 7-year-old son Manfred after his body was found at Dalston Junction Railway Station in East London. (P. 59–61).

Artist's impression of George Henry Parker during his trial at the Old Bailey in 1901. Parker was found guilty of murdering William Pearson and unlawfully wounding Rhoda King after shooting them both on a Southampton to Waterloo train. He was executed at Wandsworth Prison. (P. 62–65).

Artist's impression of John Alexander Dickman who was the last person to be hanged at Newcastle Prison, following his conviction for the murder of John Nisbet on a train journey between Newcastle and Alnmouth in 1910. (P. 72–77).

Depiction of the Ada Stone murder on a Brighton train in 1914. She was viciously stabbed to death by her partner Herbert Brooker during a drunken quarrel on a London to Brighton train near Three Bridges Station. Brooker was later hanged at Lewes Prison. (P. 77–81).

scene. Little was found on the train in the way of evidence. There were no obvious signs of a struggle having taken place, although a pair of spectacles belonging to Florence were found on the floor beneath the seat where she had been sitting. Mabel Rogers was informed of the attack the same day and she travelled from London to Eastbourne Hospital where Florence had been taken. Mabel was able to state that Florence had been in possession of a purse containing approximately £3 in cash (£168 today) when she left London. When she was admitted to hospital, the contents of her handbag were listed and her purse inside the bag was empty. The cash had been stolen. Mabel was also able to state that some items of jewellery were also missing from her person, indicating to police that a likely motive for the attack on Florence was that of robbery.

Mabel told police that the man who joined the train at Victoria was in his late twenties, of medium height and slightly built. He was wearing a brown tweed suit but was not carrying any luggage.

Police also interviewed Henry Duck, who was employed as a railway guard, working the train in question. Henry stated that he did remember something unusual occurring as the train arrived at Lewes. He was leaning out of the guard's window when he saw a passenger jump out of the train before it came to a complete stop at Lewes Station. As the train entered the station platform a man had opened a compartment door, jumped from the moving train, and ran off the end of the platform. Guard Duck shouted at the man who ignored him. The carriage that the man jumped from was, in the opinion of Duck, the same carriage where Florence Nightingale Shore was later found. He did however say that it was not wholly unusual for a passenger to alight from a train and walk off the end of that particular platform as it was sometimes used by regular passengers as an unauthorised short-cut when leaving the station. This did however suggest that the passenger who used the short-cut that day was almost certainly someone with local knowledge.

Duck gave his description of the man in question as being about 5ft 8in (173 cm) tall, athletically built, between 25 and 30 years old wearing a mackintosh coat and cap. He was not carrying any luggage. Although this description is not identical to the one given by Mabel Rogers, there are similarities, and it could well have been the same person.

Following the death of Florence Nightingale Shore, a postmortem was carried out by Bernard Spilsbury, the Home-Office pathologist. He concluded that Florence had repeatedly been struck with considerable force on the top of her head with a blunt instrument which had caused fractures to the skull and penetration of the brain itself. The impact had left an H-shaped wound in the top of the skull which indicated that the blows may have been administered using the butt of a revolver handle. Given the severity of the attack, Dr Spilsbury stated that he was surprised that her death was not instantaneous. She was in a deep coma after the attack and never regained consciousness. There were no signs of any sexual assault having taken place. The cause of death was officially recorded as coma due to fracture of the skull and injury to the brain.

Enquiries into the murder of Florence Nightingale Shore continued without much success, until an incident occurred in Eastbourne some ten days later. During the late evening of Thursday, 22 January, a large dwelling house was broken into at Arlington Road in Eastbourne. The burglar was 28-year-old man William Ernest Clements. He was 5ft 7in (170 cm) tall and slim build. After entering the house, Clements was disturbed by three members of the household domestic staff and a scuffle took place. Clements managed to break free and fled the scene, dropping a revolver on his way out. The alarm was raised, and Clements was swiftly arrested by police in a nearby street. He initially gave his name as Billy Eynon before being taken into police custody. Later, after being identified by household staff of the house he had entered, he gave his correct name to police and admitted breaking into the house.

An examination of the revolver recovered from the scene of the crime revealed what appeared to be dried blood on the butt of the revolver which Clements could not account for. William Ernest Clements quickly became a prime suspect in the murder of Florence Nightingale Shore. A search was carried out of his lodging house where a brown bloodstained suit was recovered. When interviewed, Clements denied all knowledge of the murder. He stated that he could not give an account of his whereabouts on the day of the murder or what he did during the ten days following the murder, but he denied being in London or travelling by train on the day of the murder. Unfortunately, neither Mabel Rogers nor train guard Henry

Duck was positively able to identify Clements as the man they had seen travelling on the train on the day in question.

Forensic examination proved that the dried blood found on the butt of the revolver was human, although the tests carried out at that time were unable to prove that the blood belonged to Florence Nightingale Shore.

Although the discovery of human blood groups was first announced by Karl Landsteiner in 1900, the first use of blood group evidence in English criminal cases did not occur until the 1930s, more than a decade after this murder had taken place. The suit recovered from Clements' home was also examined and proved to contain human bloodstains, but once again, they could not be linked to the murder victim.

Despite their best efforts and despite their strong suspicions, detectives were never able to prove that William Ernest Clements murdered Florence Nightingale Shore. DNA which we all take for granted today was still over sixty years away from being used to solve criminal cases in Britain and most other forms of forensic science available at that time were considered somewhat primitive by today's standards.

Although strongly suspected of having committed this offence, Clements was never charged with the murder of Florence Nightingale Shore, and the case officially remains unsolved.

Suicide Pact Leads to Murder

At the outbreak of the First World War in 1914, Lionel Edward Symonds, aged just 15, signed up to join the Royal Navy. At that time 'boy sailors' were allowed to join the Royal Navy at 15 and serve a probationary period of up to one year ashore, after which (usually on their sixteenth birthday), they were given the option of leaving or remaining in the service. If they decided to remain, they could go to sea, which Symonds did. After the war, Symonds decided to get married, so he left the service with an excellent character reference, became a family man and had two children in quick succession.

In 1921, at the age of 21, Symonds went to work as a baker's delivery roundsman for John Wall, a master baker who ran a successful business at Hersham near Walton-on-Thames in Surrey. John lived with his wife and their 14-year-old daughter Gladys, who also worked at the bakery.

As the months passed by, Lionel started to display inappropriate feelings towards Gladys, showing her affections to which she responded favourably. Over the Christmas period that year, Lionel and Gladys entered a full-blown illicit relationship, even though she was just 15 years of age. Neither her father nor her mother suspected there was anything untoward going on between them.

Early in April 1922, Gladys informed Lionel that she was expecting his child and could not bear the thought of being parted from him, so she sought his advice on what they should do. Private discussions took place between them, and they realised that if the child was born, they would have to live with the stigma it would bring upon both their families. Furthermore, Lionel was highly likely to go to prison, due to Gladys being under the age of sixteen. It was also probable that Gladys would not be allowed to keep the baby which would be given up for adoption. After much consideration, Lionel suggested they should make a 'suicide pact' so they could both die together with their unborn child. Gladys went along with the idea. After further discussion it was decided that the couple would go onto a nearby railway embankment, wait for a passing train before stepping onto the railway line in front of it.

At about 9.50 on the evening of Saturday, 22 April, during the hours of darkness, the couple climbed over a railway boundary fence at Hersham and sat together on a railway embankment, spending their last precious moments in each other's arms. A short time later they heard an approaching train in the distance. At this juncture, Lionel had a change of heart and decided he could not go through with the idea of committing suicide. Gladys on the other hand said that they had made the pact, and she was going to go through with it. She stood up and started walking up the embankment towards the railway line. Symonds grabbed Gladys by the arm and pleaded with her stop, but she pulled away from him and walked onto the railway line where she stood in the path of the oncoming train. Symonds followed her onto the track still pleading with her not to go through with it, but his words were in vain. Gladys remained standing in front of the train and was killed instantly by the locomotive. Symonds however, as if by some miracle was knocked clear of the railway line by the train but did not escape unscathed. One of his legs was amputated just below the knee by the wheels of the engine and the lower part of his other leg, including his foot was badly crushed. Although Symonds was unable to stand, he did manage to crawl to some nearby railway sidings and pull himself up into an empty carriage where he remained all night.

The following morning, the mangled body of Gladys Wall was discovered on the railway line by Henry Wheeler, a platelayer who was walking the track. Shortly afterwards, Wheeler noticed that the door of a railway carriage in the nearby railway sidings was wide open. He went to investigate and found Lionel Symonds lying on the floor inside the carriage. He appeared to have lost a considerable amount of blood from his amputated leg and was barely alive. He was rushed to hospital where he received emergency surgery to his severed leg. His other leg was so badly crushed that it could not be saved and that too, had to be amputated by doctors. Miraculously, after a lengthy stay in hospital, Symonds survived, despite having had both legs amputated just below the knees.

During the 1920s, issues surrounding the act of suicide in Britain were very controversial. Although no Act of Parliament had ever been passed making suicide a statutory criminal offence in England and Wales, suicide was generally accepted as being morally wrong and had been a criminal offence under English Common Law since the Middle Ages. Persons who committed suicide were customarily given a profane burial as well as having their property and lands forfeited by the crown.

Attempting to commit suicide was also a criminal offence under common law. If a person attempted (but failed) to take their own life, they would invariably be prosecuted for attempted suicide. The punishment normally given to such offenders was a monetary fine, a period of probation or a short term of imprisonment,

The most controversial issue in relation to suicide however involved a suicide pact. A suicide pact occurred when two or more people came to an agreement to commit suicide together.

It was a well-established principal in English law, that if two persons agreed together to commit suicide, and just one in performance of this agreement comes by his or her death, the survivor can be convicted of wilful murder. The reason for this is that the person who survived had already incited, aided, and abetted the other person to take his or her own life, in the same way as if they had incited someone to commit murder.

In view of the above, Lionel Edward Symonds was later charged with the wilful murder of Gladys Wall. Over seven months later, Symonds appeared before Mr Justice Bray at the Surrey Assizes in Guildford on Wednesday, 6 December, where he pleaded not guilty to the charge of wilful murder. Mr St John Morrow KC prosecuted on behalf of the Crown and Symonds was represented by Mr Neave KC.

With a pale face and boyish looks, the defendant presented a pathetic appearance as he was brought into court on a stretcher before being lifted, then carried by a prison officer like a baby into the dock. He was placed on a cushioned seat, with the stumps of his legs resting on another chair. Two women who had been summoned to serve on the jury trying the case were so upset by his appearance that they were excused from sitting on the jury and their places were taken by men.

Mr St John Morrow opened the case by telling the court that the girl's death was the result of her carrying out a pact to commit suicide at the instigation of the defendant. It was a type of crime which was becoming all too common. Describing it as a very sad and painful story, counsel explained that after leaving school at 14, the girl was employed in her father's bakery, where the defendant started working as a delivery roundsman.

He then explained about the relationship which developed between them and the suicide pact which followed. He continued by telling the jury that on the evening before the tragedy, the girl took part in a play at the local village hall, and she was seen speaking to Symonds in the precincts of the hall about 9.30pm. Neither of them was seen after that until the girl's body was found on the railway line the following morning. Shortly afterwards, the defendant was found badly injured in a nearby railway carriage. A bundle of letters which had been written by both Symonds to the girl and vice versa, were produced in court. The letters had been found on the railway embankment where the couple had been sitting just before Gladys committed suicide.

Mr St John Morrow, read out some of the contents of the letters, which proved beyond any doubt that a death pact between Symonds and Wall had taken place. An extract from a letter from Wall to Symons stated, 'I shall not go to the train lines because I don't wish to die like that. I would rather you killed me.' Symonds replied to Wall, also in a letter which read, 'My dear, I cannot do it myself. It must be the train, then we will both go together.' Mr St John Morrow continued to present further evidence which supported the prosecution case against Symonds.

Symonds later elected to enter the witness box and give evidence on oath in support of his own version of events that took place. He admitted to being the person responsible for the pregnancy of Gladys Wall to which he added that it had 'depressed me and depressed her'. Mr St John Morrow asked, 'Was a letter written by you to Gladys the first time that a suggestion was made about anybody killing themselves?' Symonds replied, 'Yes.' Symonds was further asked, 'Was the question of suicide discussed between you after that date?' Symonds replied, 'Yes.' Mr St. John Morrow asked, 'Was an agreement reached that you should both commit suicide in the end?' Symonds replied, 'Yes, that was on the day before it happened.'

Symonds went on to say that on the night the tragedy occurred, they left the village hall about half past nine, and he followed her through the woods to the railway embankment where they sat down. There he told her that he had changed his mind about the suicide and did not want to go through with it but was going to leave his job at the bakery instead. He further stated that he told Gladys to tell her father everything that had happened, but she just got up and started walking up the embankment towards the railway line. He said that he followed her and tried to talk her out of it, but she went onto the railway line as a train was coming. Symonds said he followed her onto the track to try to stop her, and that was the last thing he remembered.

Counsel told Symonds that the version of events he had just told the court was different to what he had told the police the day after the tragedy. He had told the police that they stood in front of the train together but only Gladys was killed. The prisoner, turning to the Judge said, 'I was helpless, my lord. I was not in a fit condition then to make any statement.' Symonds then bust into a fit of sobbing before being carried back to the dock where he was given time to recover his composure.

Mr Neave, counsel for the defence, summed up to the jury by saying that there had been a death pact, but the accused changed his mind and tried to persuade the girl not to go through with it. It was whilst trying to prevent the girl from carrying out her threat that he suffered his appalling injuries.

Mr Justice Bray then summed up the evidence, and after a deliberation by the jury of just of just eighteen minutes, they returned a guilty verdict. When asked by the judge if he had anything to say, Symonds replied ''Yes, I have not murdered anyone'. Mr Justice Bray then put on the black cap and passed a sentence of death upon the defendant, Lionel Symonds.

Following the trial, an appeal against the murder conviction was lodged by the defence counsel and the case came before a Court of Criminal Appeal on Monday 18 December. The Court of Appeal was composed of the Lord Chief Justice, Hewart, Mr Justice Darling, and Mr Justice Salter.

The Appeal Court heard that during the original trial, a question had been raised about the effect of a suicide pact. Mr Neave KC representing Mr Symonds, told the court that it was said at the trial that the parties had agreed to commit suicide. The girl was found dead on the railway line at Hersham and Symonds was found in a railway siding with injures which resulted in both his legs being amputated.

Symonds had said that he was injured whilst endeavouring to prevent Miss Wall from carrying out a threat of suicide. At the trial, Symonds was found guilty of murder and sentenced to death. Mr Neave further stated that he wished to contend that the verdict was against the weight of evidence, and that there had been a misdirection of the jury by the judge.

The Lord Chief Justice asked Mr Neave, 'Do you say there was no evidence on which the jury could convict the appellant of murder?'

Counsel Neave replied, 'No. I do not suggest that, but I suggest that the evidence produced was capable of two interpretations, and it was put by the judge to the jury as being capable of having only one interpretation. I shall submit there was evidence of a complete change of mind on the part of the defendant about committing suicide, and he decided that he would not go through with it'. He added: The prosecution had to prove that there was a suicide pact, and the pact was acted upon, although it is not disputed that there had been an earlier suicide pact.

The Lord Chief Justice: 'That means that under the well-settled and undisputed principle of English law, if two people agree to commit suicide and one of them in performance of the agreement comes by his or her death, the survivor is guilty of wilful murder?'

Counsel Neave: 'That obviously is the law as laid down.'

Lord Chief Justice: 'You are not quarrelling with that?'

Counsel Neave: 'Not for the moment. I contend that in this case the original suicide pact was not acted upon, as the defendant changed his mind, and did his best to persuade the girl from carrying it into effect.'

The Lord Chief Justice said that this was all put very clearly to the jury at the trial. Counsel Neave further argued that it was a case of 'constructive murder' because motive was implied and not expressed.

The Lord Chief Justice asked, 'If two people agree to commit suicide and one dies – can there be any doubt that the survivor has abetted and incited the other?'

Counsel Neave said that there was nothing in the summing up about incitement and argued further that the moral crime of murder, say by stabbing, was different to the moral crime of agreeing to commit suicide. The Lord Chief Justice stated that he thought the proposition was open to criticism. There might be more moral blame in the case of a suicide pact than in the case suggested by counsel.

Mr Justice Darling observed that in any event, these propositions about suicide pacts were not in the law books.

Counsel Neave later suggested that judges at different assizes had in the past taken different views on individual cases which involved suicide pacts. The view taken by Mr Justice Bray who conducted the Symonds trial was different to that of some other judges. It was tragic to think that it should depend on a particular judge who tried the case whether it should be regarded as a crime punishable by death or nine months imprisonment. He went on to say that it was the view of 75 per cent of judges that this type of crime was not one that should go to the jury as murder. Counsel Neave also suggested that the court may wish to offer an opinion that this case should be referred to the Home Secretary in view of the defendant being just 21 years of age. The Lord Chief Justice said that it was not the function of the court to do this.

In giving judgment, the Lord Chief Justice, after detailing the facts of the case, said that there was no doubt there was an agreement between the parties to commit suicide together. The prisoner's case was that he changed his mind. Mr Justice Bray in his summing up, put the issue to the jury in language that was unmistakable. His summing up was not open to criticism at all. Mr Justice Bray had correctly laid down the law on the question of a suicide agreement and murder. He explained the law clearly and accurately.

> The reason that the law should take this view is clear to all who have taken an interest in the history of English law. The court had heard today, of a suicide pact, and it was obvious there was some misapprehension as to the meaning of this part of the criminal law. The meaning was this: 'If two people agreed to commit suicide together and the bargain was acted upon, and one died, the survivor was guilty of murder. Why was this so? It was not because the one who survived had agreed to commit suicide, but that by so agreeing he incited, aided, and abetted the dead person to take his or her life, and in so doing he incited to the crime of murder and was a principal in the first degree.

The appeal was dismissed.

On Thursday 21 December, it was announced that the Right Honourable Viscount William Bridgeman, the Home Secretary, had granted Lionel Edward Symonds a reprieve against a sentence of death by hanging imposed upon him at the Surrey County Assizes on 6 December 1922, and his sentence was commuted to that of life imprisonment.

Symonds was incarcerated for eleven years before he was finally released from prison in 1934.

The acts of suicide and attempted suicide remained a criminal offence in England and Wales under Common Law until after the Second World War. A movement to have the crimes abolished began to gain support from members of the public during the 1950s. Although the Prime Minister Harold Macmillan did not support a bill to abolish the crimes, many politicians, including the Home Secretary 'Rab' Butler, did. Consequently, the Suicide Act of 1961, which decriminalised the acts of suicide and attempted suicide, was introduced and went through parliament. It received the Royal assent on 3 August 1961, after which, it became law and suicide was no longer a criminal offence in England and Wales. In 1966, an identical act was passed in Northern Ireland. Scotland however, declined to introduce similar legislation to abolish such offences, and they still exist in Scotland today.

Dropped Baby from a Carriage Window

In April 1938, Donna Rampton from London gave birth to a son Peter, who was conceived during a brief relationship with Joseph Eastwood, a married man, and a serving corporal in the Coldstream Guards. After the child was born, Donna approached Joseph and told him that as the father of her son, he would have to give her financial support to raise the child or raise the child himself. She told him that if he refused, she would go to his commanding officer and report the matter to him.

Joseph, who had been married for less than one year, was unable to give financial support for his son, so he informed his wife Marguerite of the birth, and begged her forgiveness for his affair with Donna which resulted in him fathering her child. Marguerite eventually agreed to forgive her husband for his affair and stand by him to help raise his son.

On 26 May, by prior appointment, Donna Rampton took baby Peter to a house in Charlwood Street, Pimlico, London where Marguerite Eastwood was living in rented accommodation whilst her husband was serving in the army. Donna handed Peter over to Marguerite who told her that she and Joseph, Peter's father, were going to adopt the child and look after him. That was the last time that Donna saw her son alive. Later that same evening, Marguerite Eastwood left her lodgings in Pimlico and told her landlord that she was moving to an address in Caterham, Surrey.

At about 5am the following morning, the driver of a parcels train reported seeing an object on the railway line between Barnes and Putney in South West London. A station foreman from Barnes station walked along the track and discovered what he thought to be a white bundle of rags on the track. Closer inspection found it to be the body of a young male child wearing a white vest. It was later established the child had sustained extensive injuries which included fractures to the skull, broken ribs and other injuries consistent with him having fallen from a moving train.

Police were summoned to the scene, and a murder investigation was soon underway. Enquiries revealed that a woman, carrying a young child wrapped in a white blanket had travelled on the last passenger train the previous evening, leaving Barnes Bridge Station at 10.33pm, bound for Putney. The passenger in question had booked a ticket from Barnes to Vauxhall.

An extensive murder investigation followed which resulted in the arrest of Marguerite Eastwood, aged 29 of Coulsdon Road, Caterham, Surrey. When interviewed by police, she admitted receiving baby Peter from his mother. She initially told police that she left the child in a shop doorway in Paddington, wrapped in a blanket with a note saying 'Destitute, nowhere to go. Will the finder look after it?'

Later however she retracted that statement, admitting that it was not true. She then admitted catching a bus to Barnes Station and buying a railway ticket to Vauxhall. She caught the last train and sat in an empty compartment with the child. She said that Mrs Rampton had threatened to go to her husband's commanding officer to tell him about the baby and that had nearly driven her frantic because it would have ruined his career. She told police that she had no intention of harming the baby she but didn't know what to do with it. The window in the train compartment was open so she dangled the child out of the window but did not have the courage to let go. She said, 'On the third attempt the train jerked and the child slipped from my hand. I just let it go. I will never forget the thud.'

Marguerite Eastwood subsequently appeared before the Central Criminal Court in London, charged with the wilful murder of Peter Rampton. She pleaded not guilty. Mrs Rampton, a kitchen maid and mother of the victim fainted and fell to the floor after giving her evidence which included identification of her baby's body. Marguerite Eastwood was in tears as she gave her evidence. She denied throwing the child out of the train window and said, 'I didn't mean to drop the baby. It just went.'

On 24 June, at the conclusion of the trial, the jury deliberated for just thirty minutes before returning a verdict of guilty against Marguerite Eastwood, for the wilful murder of Peter Rampton who was just four weeks old. The jury did however make the strongest possible recommendation for mercy against the death penalty being imposed.

Eastwood was then given the mandatory sentence of death by hanging, after which the trial Judge, Mr Justice du Parcq told her that the jury's strong recommendation for clemency would be forwarded at once to the appropriate authority.

Whilst sentence was being passed, Joseph Eastwood, husband of the accused, fainted at the back of the court and had to be carried out by police officers, whilst his wife was removed from the dock in a state of collapse.

Following the strong recommendation by the jury for clemency, the death sentence imposed on Marguerite Eastwood was later commuted to penal servitude for life by the Home Secretary.

Chapter 5

Mid-Twentieth Century

The Pollokshields Murders

On the evening of Monday, 10 December 1945, just three members of the railway staff were on duty at Pollokshields East Railway Station in Glasgow. Annie Withers, a station booking clerk was working a late shift, along with two railway porters, William Wright, aged 42, a senior porter in charge of the station and his assistant, Robert Gough, a junior porter, aged 15. Later that evening, the station became quiet and deserted so the three members of staff huddled around a nice warm coal fire in the Station Master's Office. It was a typical Scottish winter's evening, bitterly cold and foggy outside, but the office lights were left switched on to enable passengers to see the staff, should they require to purchase a ticket or need any assistance.

Suddenly, at about 10pm, without warning, the office door burst wide open and a young man entered brandishing a Luger semi-automatic pistol. The man pointed the weapon at Annie Withers who started screaming. A shot rang out. Annie fell to the floor. Junior Porter Gough went to her assistance and dived on top of her to shield her from the gunman. The gunman then fired a second shot at Annie to finish her off, before firing two further shots at Gough. One shot penetrated his right wrist, and the other shot was fired into his stomach. The gun was then pointed at William Wright, and as he turned away from the gunman he too was shot. Fortunately, the bullet did not penetrate Wright but grazed his body. Wright immediately fell to the floor, pretending to be dead.

The gunman then left the Station Master's Office and went next door into the booking office where the station safe was located, no doubt looking for money. He later left the station. After a short while, porter Wright got up off the floor and telephoned the local signal box, asking the signalman to raise the alarm. Wright who was bleeding quite heavily, staggered onto the platform outside and the police and ambulance services arrived a short time later. Annie Withers was conveyed by ambulance to the nearby Victoria Hospital where she was pronounced dead on arrival. William Wright and Robert Gough were also taken there. Sadly, Robert Gough who was in a critical condition, died two days later due to his injuries. William Wright made a full recovery, having been lucky enough to only have a glancing wound. He was only able to give a vague description of the attacker to detectives; a white male, aged early twenties, medium build, medium height with a pale, thin face. He was smartly dressed in a light-coloured raincoat and wearing a brown hat.

Detective Superintendent William Ewing took charge of the murder enquiry, and several fingerprints left by the gunman were found in the Station Master's Office. Unfortunately, they could not be matched to any known offender which suggested that the offender was not known to police. Despite a thorough search of the area, the murder weapon was never found.

An audit check carried out at the station booking office revealed that the only property to have been stolen was a staff wage packet containing £4 3s 6d (£200 today).

In the weeks that followed, police had little success in the double-murder investigation, until in October 1946, some ten months later, police received an anonymous tip-off that a man called Charles Templeman Brown, a railway locomotive fireman who lived at 19 Brisbane Street, Glasgow, just over a mile from Pollokshields East Railway Station, was the owner of a 9mm German manufactured Luger semi-automatic pistol which was at his home. Detectives visited the address, but Brown was not at home. His mother told police that her son was working trains between Glasgow and Carlisle, and she did not know when he would be back. The detectives then left a message with Mrs Brown to ask her son to contact the police when he returned home.

On Wednesday, 9 October, Charles Brown received the message from his mother that detectives had visited the house looking for him and wanted him to contact the police. He immediately started to panic. Fearing that he was about to be apprehended for the murders, he took the pistol from his bedroom where he had hidden it. He then went for a walk with the intention of committing suicide but could not go through with it. In a complete state of fear and panic, he did not know what to do until he saw a uniformed police constable standing in the street. PC John Byrne was on point duty directing road traffic and was flabbergasted when Brown approached him, handed over the Luger pistol, together with a box of ammunition, before confessing to committing the Pollokshields murders. Brown was immediately arrested and taken into custody.

On 10 December, exactly one year after the murder of Annie Withers and Robert Gough, Charles Templeman Brown, aged 21, appeared before Lord Carmont at the High Court in Glasgow where he pleaded not guilty to the crimes. The defence argued that Brown was a schizophrenic, and he should be acquitted on grounds of diminished responsibility at the time of the murders. The prosecution produced evidence showing that there was nothing to suggest that Brown suffered from any mental illness and on 13 December he was found guilty of the double murder and sentenced to death by hanging. The sentence was due to be carried out at Barlinnie Prison, Glasgow on Friday, 3 January 1947. On 30 December, however, a petition for a reprieve of his death sentence was upheld, and his sentence was commuted to one of life imprisonment. Brown never revealed why he committed the crimes, but his mother told detectives that during his teens he was a 'Walter Mitty' type character who hero-worshipped Adolf Hitler. He was also envious of boys slightly older than himself who joined the army, fought during the war, and then returned home boasting about the excitement of war and the number of German soldiers they had supposedly killed.

Whilst incarcerated in prison, Brown did show some remorse for his crimes and became a practicing Christian. He was released from prison after serving eleven years of his life sentence before gaining employment as a salesman for a tyre company. He worked hard, joined a church choir, and became a model son to his mother. Eighteen months after his release from prison, Brown was killed when a car which he was driving was involved in a serious accident on the road between Stirling and Dunblane. The date of the accident was 10 December 1957, exactly twelve years to the day that he committed his brutal crimes.

Murder of a Railway Booking Clerk

In May 1950, Geoffrey Charles Dean, aged 26, a married man with a small child, started working as a booking clerk at his local village railway station in Ash Vale which lies on the border between Surrey and Hampshire. Geoffrey lived a quiet but enjoyable family life in the sedate village until Friday, 22 August 1952, when he was stabbed to death in a frenzied attack whilst performing his duties inside the station booking office. His attacker was a railway locomotive fireman by the name of John James Alcott, aged just 21 who was also married and based at Hither Green steam locomotive depot in South-East London (the depot closed in October 1961).

It appears that John James Alcott, a locomotive fireman had promised his wife that he would take her to France on holiday during August 1952 when he was booked to take a two-week summer holiday break from work. He was able to use his railway staff travel facilities to travel by train and ferry to France free of charge for himself and his wife. Upon arriving in France, the couple intended to book hotel accommodation for the duration of their holiday.

On the morning of Monday, 18 August, Alcott informed his wife that he was going to Hither Green depot where he worked to collect his holiday pay so they could start their annual holiday and travel to France the following day. His wife was thrilled at the idea, and she spent the day preparing and packing the luggage.

That was the last time she saw her husband until after his arrest. Alcott did not return home that day, but instead, he travelled to Aldershot and whilst he was there, he purchased a Bowie-type sheath knife. Later, he booked into a hotel for the night where it is assumed that he planned a way to get some extra money, presumably to pay for the holiday. The purchase of the Bowie knife suggested that he may have been planning to use it, or threatening to use it, possibly with evil intent.

The next sighting of Alcott was at about 11.15am on Wednesday, 20 August when he visited Ash Vale station booking office and made enquiries about the times of boat-trains running between Victoria Station in London and Dover. He apparently spent that night in Clapham but arrived back at Ash Vale station by train at 6.30am the following morning and started talking to a railway porter on the platform. He introduced himself as a fellow railway worker and started talking in general about the railways. At about 7am, the porter told Alcott that it was his breakfast time, and he invited Alcott into the porter's room for a cup of tea which Alcott accepted. Whilst inside the porter's room, Alcott started to clean his fingernails with the knife he had bought in Aldershot three days earlier, and when the porter asked why he was carrying a sheath knife, he said that he had bought it for his nephew. After chatting with other members of the station staff, Alcott left the station but returned at about 5pm that afternoon.

On this occasion, Alcott went directly to the booking office and spoke to the booking clerk (not the murder victim Geoffrey Dean). He showed the booking clerk his railway pass and asked if he could use the railway telephone as he needed to phone his depot at Hither Green. The booking clerk allowed him into the office, and he appeared to use the telephone.

Alcott then remained in the booking office some considerable time, chatting with the booking clerk, and he hung around until 7.45pm when the booking clerk told him that he was 'shutting shop' as the booking office closed at 8pm. It was usual practice for some blank tickets and date stamps to be handed over to a senior night porter at about 7.45pm to enable him to issue tickets from the station waiting room to any passengers wanting to travel after the booking office closed at 8pm. It only became apparent later that the reason Alcott had spent so much time at Ash Vale Station that week was to observe the movements and duties of the station staff, and particularly the booking clerks, to enable him to carry out an audacious robbery at the station booking office.

On the following Friday, at approximately 7.30pm, booking clerk Geoffrey Dean was on duty in the booking office when Alcott again turned up at the station. Dean was unaware that Alcott had previously visited the station but after being shown his railway staff pass, he allowed Alcott into the booking office, so he could use the railway telephone to phone his depot at Hither Green. Once again, Alcott purported to make the telephone call, then remained inside the office chatting to Dean who closed the ticket serving hatch at about 7.45pm, after passing the blank tickets and date stamps through the hatch to the night porter who took them to the waiting room. The events which followed are subject to some speculation.

As Dean went to put the takings out of the cash drawer into the booking office safe, he was viciously attacked by Alcott, who used the Bowie knife to inflict multiple and fatal stab wounds on his body. Alcott stabbed Dean no less than twenty times, before stealing the contents of the cash drawer and the contents of the safe. The cash stolen amounted to £168 in total (approximately £7,200. today). After leaving the booking office, Alcott locked the booking office behind him, leaving Dean inside the office, either dead or dying in a pool of his own blood.

Shortly before 9pm that evening, the railway porter who was on duty noticed that although the booking office was locked and appeared to be empty, the lights had been left on. This gave him a cause for concern, so he climbed onto a windowsill and peered through the glass window, where he saw Dean lying on the floor next to the office safe, the door of which was wide open. The Station Master was called out from his home nearby and immediately went to the station. The booking office door was forced open and upon entering the office, the Station Master saw the body of Geoffrey Dean lying next to the open safe. His face and body were covered in blood, and he appeared to be dead. Some paper bags containing small denomination copper coins were on the floor next to the body, together with the safe keys. Police were immediately summoned to the railway station and a police murder incident room was set up in one of the station's waiting rooms.

A murder investigation was quickly in progress and the following morning a systematic check was carried out of hotels and guest houses in and around the Aldershot area. During these enquiries, police visited a lodging house in Victoria Road, Aldershot, where they discovered a blood-stained jacket in a first-floor bedroom. Inside the pocket of the jacket were two passports in the name of James Alcott and his wife. Police remained at the premises all day until, at 11pm that night, when James Alcott returned to the lodgings where he was arrested on suspicion of murder and robbery. When searched he was in possession of £110 in notes (£4,700. today), secured with a rubber band which he admitted was part of the money stolen from the booking office. Alcott also admitted stabbing Geoffrey Dean and told police that he had hidden the knife in the chimney of the room they were in. Officers immediately recovered the murder weapon from the chimney of the bedroom and Alcott was taken into custody.

A postmortem was later carried out on the murder victim which established that the attack had been carried out ferociously with a stab wound behind the right ear having severed the jugular vein and the lingual artery. There were nine stab wounds in the victim's back, seven in the front of the chest, one of which had been carried out with such force that it had passed through the breastbone and into the heart itself. There were also stab wounds to the face, abdomen, arms, and legs. In addition, police forensic evidence matched blood found on the murder weapon and the defendant's clothing to that of the victim. The murder enquiries carried out were a joint operation between the Surrey Constabulary, the Hampshire Constabulary, and the British Transport Commission Police, with Detective Superintendent Roberts (Surrey Constabulary) heading the investigation.

On Wednesday, 20 November, James John Alcott, of Eltham Palace Road, Eltham near Greenwich in London, appeared before Mr Justice Finnemore at the Surrey Assizes, Kingston, charged with the wilful murder of Geoffrey Charles Green and robbery at Ash Vale railway station on 22 August. He pleaded not guilty to the charges. Mr John Flowers QC conducted the prosecution, and Mr C.G. DuCann represented the accused.

The facts concerning the visits to Ash Vale railway station made by the defendant in the days prior to the offence were not disputed by the defence, neither was the stabbing of Geoffrey Charles Dean, nor the stealing of the cash from the booking office. The defence placed before the court was that at the actual time of the murder and the robbery, Alcott was under a 'defect of reason', due to disease of the mind. However, after the case had been presented before the jury, the judge, Mr Justice Finnemore, in his summing up, told them: 'It is my duty to tell you that there was no evidence of insanity, or evidence that Alcott was suffering from any defect of reason, or that he did not know quite well what he was doing.' The jury subsequently found James John Alcott guilty as charged.

After the verdict was delivered, Judge Finnemore told Alcott 'The jury has found you guilty on evidence they could not possibly ignore.' He then passed the mandatary sentence for murder, that of death by hanging. On

2 January 1953, James John Alcott, aged 22, was executed at Wandsworth Prison in London. The executioner was Albert Pierrepoint.

It later transpired that after leaving school, James Alcott had joined the British Grenadier Guards. Whilst serving in Germany in 1949, Alcott got into an argument with Peter Helm, a German citizen employed as a night watchman. Alcott viciously beat Helm with a fire extinguisher and an empty whiskey bottle before stabbing him to death in a frenzied attack with a knife. After being tried before a military court-martial in the City of Bielefeld, Germany, Alcott was found guilty of murdering Helm and sentenced to death. On the advice of the Judge Advocate General's Department at the war office, George VI refused to formally confirm the sentence, which was a requirement in law before it could be carried out. This resulted in the conviction being quashed. Alcott then returned to Britain, left the armed forces, and became a locomotive fireman on the railway. Had the first death sentence on Alcott, handed out in Germany been imposed, the brutal murder of booking clerk Geoffrey Dean would never have taken place.

Polish Countess Stabbed on the Underground

Teresa Lubienska (nee Skarzynski), born 1884, was a Polish aristocrat who was a political prisoner during the Second World War, after being seized from her home in Poland in 1942 and interned in Ravensbrück Concentration Camp in northern Germany. The camp was Germany's largest female-only concentration camp, housing over 120,000 inmates from all over Europe, in which it is thought that up to 90,000 prisoners died from starvation, illness or execution between 1939 and 1945. Countess Lubienska herself experienced torture, starvation and severe illness whilst confined to the camp, but somehow, she miraculously survived for three long years before her release, after which she fled to England at the age of 61. She eventually arrived in London where she settled and lived a modest life, alone in a single room in Kensington before finding friends, primarily amongst the Polish community. Her husband Edward, a Russian citizen was stabbed to death in 1919 during the Bolshevik Revolution and her only son, a Polish soldier, was killed the start of the Second World War.

On 24 May 1957, Teresa, who was then aged 73, visited a friend's house in Florence Road, Ealing in West London. She left the house that evening in company with another friend, Father Krzyzanowski, a Polish priest, and they caught a train together from Ealing Broadway Station on the London Underground. Father Krzyzanowski alighted from the train at Earl's Court Station, and Teresa alighted at the next station which was Gloucester Road.

At about 10.20pm, not long after getting off her train, Teresa was seen staggering along the deserted eastbound Piccadilly Line platform of Gloucester Road Station by Emanuel Akinyemi, the station foreman. She was in a very distressed state and uttered the words, 'I've been knifed, I've been knifed.' There was blood flowing profusely from the left side of her chest. She was assisted into a lift by Akinyemi and taken to the station booking hall at street level where an ambulance was summoned.

Teresa was rushed to St Mary Abbott's Hospital but died a few hours later. She was never able to give details as to what had happened to her. It was later confirmed that she had been stabbed five times in the chest, stomach and back, which had ultimately led to her death. She was subsequently buried at Brompton Cemetery in London.

An extensive murder enquiry was carried out into the wilful murder of Teresa Lubienska but without success. The motive for the murder was never established. One theory was that Teresa may have been stabbed following an altercation with a gang of youths who she had rebuked for their unruly conduct or bad behaviour, as it was relatively common for unruly behaviour fuelled by alcohol to occur on the London Underground network late at night. Robbery seemed an unlikely motive, as her money and personal belongings were all intact. During the murder investigation, approximately 2,000 house-to-house enquiries were conducted by police and over 18.000 people were interviewed. No witnesses to the incident ever came forward and there were never any suspects named in connection with the murder. The case remains unsolved.

Three Mile Journey of Terror

On Wednesday, 7 April 1965, 31-year-old Mrs Enid Wheeler boarded the 12.24pm passenger train at Aldershot in Hampshire to travel just 3 miles to the next station at Ash Vale where she lived. Ash Vale lies on the border between Hampshire and Surrey. The journey time between the two stations was only four minutes. Enid, a part-time chemist's assistant, had been working at Boots Pharmacy in Aldershot that day but finished work at midday due to Wednesday being early closing.

Unbelievably, during that short four-minute train ride, a frenzied attack was carried out on Enid in which she was repeatedly stabbed before being thrown from the moving train. The motive for the attack was never established. The train in question was a local service from Guildford to Ascot and consisted of just two coaches. There was no more than a handful of passengers on the train at the time.

The first indication that an incident had occurred on the train was discovered as it pulled into Ash Vale Station, and a railway porter noticed that one of the train compartment doors was swinging wide open. He hurried along the station platform and found that there were no occupants in the compartment, although an unattended white plastic holdall was on one of the seats.

The porter immediately telephoned Richard Powell, the Station Master at Aldershot and reported the matter to him. Powell responded quickly by closing the railway line between Aldershot and Ash Vale. He quickly mustered a special train, which conveyed him and two other railway staff members towards Ash Vale, making an examination of the track along the way. As the train approached Ash Vale, Enid Wheeler was found lying on the side of the track, just 300 yards from Fir Acre Road, where she lived with her husband Derek. Enid was covered in blood, emanating from what appeared to be stab wounds on her body. She was barely alive, so Station Master Powell gave her the 'kiss of life' until the arrival of an ambulance. Enid was conveyed to the Cambridge Military Hospital in Aldershot but died shortly after her arrival.

Detective Chief Superintendent John Place of the Hampshire Constabulary immediately launched a murder enquiry into the death of Enid Wheeler and during a search of the railway line near to where her body was found, Detective Constable Henson recovered a bloodstained knife bearing fingerprints, which was lying in the grass on the railway embankment. A subsequent forensic examination of the knife confirmed it to be the murder weapon.

Several sets of fingerprints were also lifted from inside the railway carriage where the attack on Mrs Wheeler had taken place. Evidence would later be presented in court showing that some of these fingerprints, and those on the murder weapon, belonged to a man called Patrick Jenner who quickly became a suspect in this case. Later that day, detectives arrested Patrick John Jenner, aged 21, a single unemployed labourer who lived with his parents at Downshill Cottage, Runfold in Surrey. Jenner was conveyed to Aldershot Police Station.

At 11.10pm the same evening, Detective Chief Inspector Owen Breach from Weybridge Police Station in Surrey visited Aldershot Police Station in company with detective Harry Gibbs of Woking where they conducted an interview with Jenner. DCI Breach told Jenner that they had just come from Aldershot mortuary where they had seen the body of Enid Wheeler who had died due to stab wounds on her body. He informed Jenner that she had been stabbed to death in a railway carriage and that her body was recovered alongside the railway line between Aldershot and Ash Vale.

DCI Breach further stated that he had reason to believe that he (Jenner) had travelled in the same railway carriage. Jenner was cautioned and it was alleged that he replied, 'Oh, good God, is she dead?' DCI Breach asked Jenner if he could throw any light on her death. Jenner said, 'Not me. I have not got the guts to kill a cat. I didn't kill her.' Jenner was then taken to Farnham Police Station in Surrey, pending further enquiries.

The following morning, Thursday, 8 April, Doctor Keith Mount, a home office pathologist, carried out a postmortem on the body of Mrs Wheeler which confirmed that she had received seventeen stab wounds to her body. This he confirmed, resulted in her death. At 5.15pm that afternoon, at Farnham Police Station, Patrick John Jenner was again seen by Detective Chief Inspector Breach who formally charged him with the wilful murder of Enid Wheeler. When cautioned and asked if he wished to say anything, he replied, 'Not until I have seen a solicitor.'

On Friday, 9, Jenner appeared before Farnham Magistrates where he was represented by a local solicitor, Mr Stedman, who made no objections to an application that his client be remanded in custody. The chairman of the bench, Mr B.H. Dymock, remanded Jenner in custody to reappear before the court on 15 April 1965 when he was committed to stand trial at the Surrey Assizes. He remained in custody, pending the trial.

On Thursday, 8 July, Patrick John Jenner appeared before the Surrey Assize Court at Kingston upon Thames, where he pleaded not guilty to the wilful murder of Enid May Wheeler. Under cross-examination, however, he did admit to having travelled on the train in question. After the evidence had been presented it took the jury just twenty-eight minutes to find the defendant guilty by a unanimous decision.

The judge, Mr Justice Fenton-Atkinson, told Jenner, 'The jury has found you guilty on overwhelming evidence of a singularly vicious and horrible murder.' Jenner was then sentenced to life imprisonment.

Body Found in Disused Railway Tunnel

Sometime in 1962, schoolboy, Douglas Leslie Smith, aged 16, who lived in Thomas Lane, Knotty Ash, Liverpool, met Phillip John Owen who was ten years younger than himself, at just 6 years of age. Owen lived just half a mile away from Smith, at Jubilee Avenue with his mother and stepfather. Despite their age difference, a close friendship developed between them. Phillip's mother did not entirely approve of the relationship because of the age gap between the two boys, but she did not mention the fact and a close relationship between the boys developed over the next three years.

On 11 October 1965, Douglas Smith, who was then aged nineteen and working as a hospital porter, visited the home of Phillip and spoke to Mrs Owen, Phillip's mother. He informed Mrs Owen that her son Phillip had been spreading nasty rumours about him, which were circulating around Knotty Ash Primary School where her son was a pupil, and he asked her to put a stop to it. Mrs Owen said she would speak to her son about it, but she asked Douglas to stop seeing her son altogether, as she did not approve of the relationship because of the age difference between them.

On Monday, 18 October, between 5.50pm and 6pm, Phillip Owen decided to slip out of his home, whilst his mother's back was turned as he had secretly arranged to meet up with Douglas Smith at Broad Street Railway Station. In the meantime, Smith visited a shop in Jubilee Avenue where he bought some fireworks. After the boys met at Broad Street Railway Station, they decided to let the fireworks off in a nearby disused railway tunnel so they could listen to the echoes made by the exploding fireworks. At about 6.45pm, both boys were seen walking along a railway embankment towards the disused railway tunnel. Phillip Owen never returned home that evening, and his worried parents contacted the police to report him missing.

The following morning police started making enquires and searching for the missing boy, until at 10.30 am on Wednesday 20 October, two days after Phillip went missing, his body was discovered by two police officers, lying inside the disused railway tunnel, about 30 yards (27.5 meters) from the tunnel entrance.

The short trousers which he had been wearing were around his ankles, together with his underpants. There were no visible signs of injury to his body, although a later postmortem revealed that his death had been caused by strangulation. The remains of some spent fireworks were found inside the tunnel, some distance away from the body, together with two unexploded fireworks.

At 12.50pm that day, Douglas Leslie Smith, aged 19 was arrested by police outside his home and he was found to be in possession of eight fireworks which were identical to those found inside the railway tunnel. He was conveyed to Eaton Road Police Station where he later made a written statement, in which he admitted killing Owen by strangulation with his scarf. He was subsequently charged with wilful murder.

On Friday 28 January 1966, Douglas Leslie Smith appeared before Liverpool Crown Court where the judge, Mr Justice Lyell committed him to Rampton High Security Hospital in Nottinghamshire for an unlimited period after the jury found him not guilty of wilful murder, but guilty of manslaughter on the grounds of diminished responsibility.

Chapter 6

IRA Murder and Terror Campaigns

Irish Republican Army at War with Britain

In January 1939, the IRA Council (the decision-making body of the Irish Republican Army), issued a war ultimatum to the British government to withdraw all British military personnel from Ireland. The government ignored the ultimatum, which resulted in the IRA leaders making a declaration of war against Britain. They decided to conduct a bombing campaign on mainland Britain which was known as the S-plan (Sabotage plan). The object of the S-plan was twofold: to create panic and fear amongst the population (rather than deaths or casualties); and to cause disruption by damaging or destroying Britain's infrastructure with the use of explosives.

Their targets included military establishments, government buildings, power installations, communications, and transport networks, which included the railways.

1939 was a fateful year in British history, as the IRA bombing campaign gathered momentum, people were already making preparations for the outbreak of the Second World War, which started in September of that year. The railways played a vital role in the war effort and as autumn approached, the railways were working to full capacity, transporting troops and munitions to docks and harbours nationwide on a massive scale, whilst at the same time, having to contend with IRA atrocities.

Numerous S-plan atrocities were committed by the IRA that year which caused widespread disruption to the railway network. There were numerous casualties and there seemed to be little or no regard for the death or injuries sustained by innocent people who just happened to be in the wrong place at the wrong time.

Bombs on the London Underground

On Friday, 10 February 1939, two bombs exploded at Leicester Square and Tottenham Court Road Underground Stations in London, causing extensive damage to both stations. Seven people were injured in the explosions, two of them seriously. Both bombs were concealed inside suitcases which had been deposited in left luggage offices at each of the stations the previous day, and they had been fitted with time fuses set to explode between 2am and 6am the following morning. Had the explosions been timed to go off in the rush hours just a few hours later, it is likely there would have been a large-scale loss of life. The devices used in the explosions, were identical to some which had previously been used by the IRA to blow up customs huts on the Northern Ireland border.

Railwayman Foiled an Attempt to Blow Up a Bridge

Railway signalling engineer Mr H. West from Greenford in London was hailed a hero after foiling what was believed to be an IRA attempt to blow up a bridge on the Metropolitan Railway during the early hours of the morning on Saturday, 4 March 1939.

West had been sent to carry out emergency repairs on a set of faulty signal points which were located near a railway bridge, spanning Park Avenue, not far from Willesden Green Railway Station. He arrived on site just after 2.30am and the whole of the surrounding area was deserted and quiet. Shortly before 3am, West saw the headlights of a car being driven along Park Avenue and as it approached the bridge, it slowed down and stopped underneath it. A short while later, four men alighted from the vehicle and one of them opened the car boot. West watched as two of the men lifted a large box from the vehicle and carried it to the railway boundary fence. One of the men climbed over the fence, then the other man passed him the box before climbing over the fence himself. The first man started carrying the box up the railway embankment towards the underside of the railway bridge with the second man following a few yards behind. In the meantime, the other two men had removed a second, similar sized box from the car, lifted it over the fence, and they too started ascending the embankment with one of the men carrying the box.

West then decided to see what the men were up to, so he made his way from the top of the bridge down the embankment towards the men, until he intercepted the man who was walking in front of the others and carrying one of the boxes. He asked the man where he was going but the man just dropped the box and threw a punch at West. A struggle ensued and both men started to roll further down the embankment. The man who had been carrying the box suddenly pushed West away and shouted, 'Shoot the bastard.' West looked up and a second man who was standing just a few metres away pulled a revolver out of his pocket and pointed it towards him. West saw a flash, followed by a loud bang. Fortunately, the shot missed, so West started to scamper back up the embankment as another shot was fired at him. The second shot also missed; he had a lucky escape. West then turned around to see if he was still being chased and he saw that the four men had scurried back down the embankment to their car taking the boxes with them. He then heard the car start up and watched as it sped away from the scene. Upon reaching the top of the embankment, West ran to a lineside telephone and reported the incident to the signalman, who contacted the police. Several police cars quickly arrived at the bridge and West informed them of what had happened. Police then made an extensive search of the area, but the men had gone to ground and were never apprehended. The actions of Mr West may well have prevented a serious catastrophe.

Bombing Campaign Disrupts the Midlands

On Sunday, 2 July 1939, mayhem occurred on the London, Midland, and Scottish Railway, after a total of seven different bombs exploded at various railway stations in the Midland counties of England, during a three hour period in the early hours of the morning. The railway in the Midlands was closed completely until police were satisfied that there were no more explosive devices. When the railway re-opened, severe disruptions and delays to services continued for the rest of the day.

The following railway stations were directly affected: Leicester London Road; Birmingham New Street; Derby; Stratford-upon-Avon; Nottingham; Coventry Central; Leamington Spa (Milverton).

The first explosion took place at Derby Station just before 3am, as Benjamin Paggett, aged 63, an attendant on duty in the left luggage and parcels office, was drinking a cup of tea when he heard a hissing sound and noticed a blue flame emerge from a suitcase. He made a dash for the door and just managed to clear the exit of the building when a massive explosion occurred. Paggett received some minor injuries and was badly shaken. The building was extensively damaged and several items of luggage, together with numerous parcels inside the office were damaged or destroyed. Police quickly arrived and sealed off the station before making a thorough search of it. There were no other explosive devices, and no suspects were found on or in the vicinity of the station.

Less than an hour later, an almost identical explosion occurred at Birmingham New Street Station when a metal canister which had earlier been deposited in the left luggage/parcel's office exploded. The doors and glass roof of the office were blown off and a large quantity of passenger luggage and railway parcels inside the office was damaged or destroyed. The left luggage attendant Phillip Willis had a remarkable escape. He was inside the office when he saw a flash, followed by a flame in the back of the room, so he ran out of the office to sound the fire alarm. Suddenly, there was a massive explosion. He later said, 'I am a very lucky chap. If I had been in there a few seconds longer, I would have been blown to bits.' Several windows of a train standing in the station platform were also shattered by the blast, such was the severity of the explosion. Fortunately, there were no serious injuries to any of the passengers inside the train.

Copycat explosions also occurred at Coventry, Stratford, and Nottingham Stations in the early hours, at a time when all three stations were almost deserted. As in the other explosions, items of luggage and parcels were destroyed or damaged, and the left luggage/parcels office buildings suffered severe structural damage. When the Nottingham bomb went off, the sound of the explosion could be heard by residents in their homes up to 2 miles away.

Leicester Station was deserted at 3.30 that morning, apart from two men, Charles Venn, aged 61, a ticket collector and Mr Thompson of Willow Street, Leicester, who were both in the station booking hall when an explosion occurred. Ticket collector Venn was in conversation with

Thompson who was awaiting his wife's arrival at the station by train. Suddenly, the men heard a sizzling noise, followed by smoke pouring from a suitcase which had been left in a wooden cubicle used by the ticket collectors alongside the ticket gate leading to the platforms. Suspecting it could be a bomb, both men dashed for safety, but the device exploded before they could reach the booking hall exit doors. They were conveyed to hospital. Venn was treated for serious injuries to his left arm, legs, and face. Thompson was treated for more minor injuries. The explosion demolished the ticket collector's cubicle and caused severe damage inside the booking hall from which eleven truckloads of debris were later removed. The explosion was heard 4 miles away.

The last of the explosive devices that morning was detonated at 5.45am, at Leamington Spa Station in Warwickshire. The explosion caused a fire to break out which was quickly extinguished by station staff. Some passengers were standing on the station platform when the explosion occurred and several suffered the effects of shock, but luckily, no injuries were sustained. Again, extensive damage occurred to station buildings, in particular the left luggage/parcel's office which was almost entirely demolished, whilst some of the contents inside were badly damaged, and others completely destroyed.

The explosive devices used in all the above incidents were almost identical and were all triggered by a timing mechanism. The bombs had been deposited at each of the railway stations on Saturday, 1 July and set to explode at various times between 2am and 6am the following morning. It was apparent that the explosions were intended to cause as much structural damage and disruption as possible to the railway, whilst at the same time trying to avoid multiple deaths and injuries to railway staff and members of the public. The bombs were all detonated to explode at a time when the stations were almost deserted. Had the explosions taken place during the daytime, particularly during peak traffic hours, the potential loss of life and serious injury to individuals may well have been colossal.

Bomb Explodes at Wolverhampton

At 5.30am on Monday, 17 July 1939, two-weeks after the seven explosions on the Midland railway, another suitcase containing explosives, exploded in the left luggage office at Wolverhampton Station on the GWR, causing considerable damage to the building and its contents. All the windows were blown out of the building and there was extensive structural damage to the roof. The station platforms were covered with broken glass. Fortunately, the station was almost deserted when the bomb went off and there were no casualties.

Bomb Fatality at King's Cross

On Wednesday, 26 July 1939, staff and passengers were not so lucky when another IRA bomb went off at King's Cross Station, on the LNER. On this occasion, unlike previous IRA bombs, the device was not timed to explode in the early hours of the morning, when the station was quiet, but at 1.40pm in the afternoon.

Once again, extensive damage was caused by the explosion, which on this occasion sadly resulted in the death of Dr Donald Campbell, aged 35, a university lecturer from Edinburgh. He was killed instantly by the explosion and fifteen other people were injured, some of them seriously. Once again, the bomb was contained inside a suitcase which had been deposited in the left luggage office the previous day.

Bomb at Victoria Station

A mere eight hours after the bombing atrocity occurred at King's Cross Station, a similar explosion occurred on the Southern Railway at Victoria Station in London just after 9.30pm. A total of five railway employees were seriously injured when another bomb was detonated in the left luggage office.

As a direct result of these two latest explosions at King's Cross and Victoria Stations, a nationwide policy was immediately introduced at railway stations throughout Britain. Staff were instructed, and notices were exhibited at all stations, stating that passengers must open all luggage for inspection before it would be accepted at any left luggage office.

A combination of the railway luggage inspection policy and a horrific explosion which occurred in Coventry on 25 August 1939 did dramatically reduce the IRA railway bombing campaign. The Coventry bomb explosion was not targeted at a railway location, but due to its significance in the overall history of the S-plan bombing campaign the details are included in this chapter.

Outrage Following Coventry Bombing

The IRA bombings on mainland Britain reduced dramatically following a massive explosion which occurred in a busy Coventry shopping centre at 2.30pm on Friday, 25 August 1939. A bicycle with pannier bags packed with high explosives was left outside a shop, shortly before being detonated. A mammoth explosion caused considerable damage to no less than forty-three business premises spread over a wide area of the city.

Five people were killed in the explosion and over fifty were injured, twelve of them seriously. Following the massive explosion, there was widespread panic in the city as people feared the Second World War had started, until it was confirmed that the blast had been caused by an IRA bomb.

The Coventry bombing was the last straw for many people, and caused anger, outrage, and Irish resentment throughout much of Britain. This prompted an official announcement by the IRA, that the mainland bombing campaign in Britain would be wound down. Although the S-plan campaign officially continued until March 1940, only a handful of IRA incidents occurred after the Coventry bombing and there was no further loss of life.

Two men, Peter Barnes aged 32 and James McCormick (Alias James Richards), aged 29, were both arrested for the murder of the five people killed in the Coventry bombing, and following a trial at Birmingham Assizes on 14 December 1939, they were found guilty by a jury who deliberated for just thirty minutes. Both men were hanged at Winson Green Prison, Birmingham on 7 February 1940. Shortly after the sentences had been carried out, the IRA S-plan bombing campaign came to an end.

IRA Bombing Campaign 1969-97

After the S-plan bombing campaign came to an end in March 1940, the railways of Britain did not undergo any further encounters with the IRA until in 1969, when the IRA decided to conduct protest marches and an armed paramilitary campaign in Northern Ireland and England, which was once again aimed at ending British rule in Northern Ireland.

On 30 January 1972, twenty-six unarmed civilians were shot by British soldiers during a protest march at Derry in Northern Ireland. Fourteen civilians died and the event later became known as the Bloody Sunday Massacre. This resulted in the IRA carrying out a retaliation in mainland Britain.

On 22 February 1972, just three weeks after the massacre, a car laden with explosives was detonated outside the officer's mess at an army base in Aldershot. There were no officers inside the mess when the explosion occurred, but seven civilian workers were killed in the blast. This was just the start of a campaign of terror which was to last for over two decades.

Rather surprisingly, the railway network did not suffer IRA retribution at the start of this new campaign. The reason may have been that since the S-plan campaign of 1939, an extensive road network, including motorways, had been constructed in Britain and the railway did not play as important a role for transporting goods and passengers as it had done in the past.

By the 1970s, vast amount of freight was being transported by road and many people were using cars and other forms of road vehicles as a means of transport. Instead of targeting the railways, the IRA concentrated their bombing campaign elsewhere, leaving the railway network untouched for over eighteen months, although sadly this was about to change, as people in London where the railways still played a vital role in transporting commuters and other passengers, were about to find out.

Bomb Explosions at King's Cross and Euston Stations

The first railway station to incur the wrath of the IRA in this new campaign was King's Cross mainline station, when at 12.30pm on Monday, 10 September 1973, a bomb exploded without warning in a disused booking office near platform eight. Six people were injured, one of them seriously. One of the victims described the bomber as a young man in his late teens, height 5ft 2in, slim build, dark hair with a slightly tanned complexion. He was wearing a white shirt, blue short-sleeved V-neck sweater, light grey trousers, and black shoes. He was never apprehended.

At 1.10pm the same day, a man with an Irish accent telephoned the Press Association in London, warning that another bomb had been planted at Euston Station and was due to go off at any time soon. Just three minutes later, the bomb exploded in the station snack bar, injuring five people,

Another problem which police had to contend with throughout this latest bombing campaign was the vast number of hoax bomb calls being made. Just to give an example, when the above-mentioned bombs exploded at King's Cross and Euston, four bomb hoax calls were received the same day, stating that bombs had also been planted at Victoria Station, King's Cross Underground Station, Charing Cross Station and a second bomb at Euston Station due to go off later that evening. In each instance, the stations were closed, evacuated, and searched before passengers could be allowed back. These severe disruptions to the rail network and subsequent delays to train services were due entirely to hoax bomb calls being made to the authorities.

Bomb Planted on a Passenger Train

On Thursday, 4 March 1976, a passenger train left Sevenoaks Station in Kent at 7.49am, bound for Cannon Street Station in London. The ten-coach train was packed with between 650 and 750 commuters. It arrived at Cannon Street on time at 8.35am. After all the passengers had alighted, the empty train pulled away from the platform, destined for the railway sidings when there was a massive explosion. One of the coaches on the train was completely ripped apart with the roof blown off. Just a few minutes earlier, the coach had been packed with over seventy passengers. Although there were no casualties in the empty train where the explosion occurred, another train, the 8.43am Cannon Street to Gravesend train, departed Cannon Street Station at about the same time and was travelling alongside the empty train when the bomb went off. Sadly, several passengers inside the coach of the Gravesend train which took the brunt of the blast from the explosion, were injured and eight of them had to be conveyed to hospital. Fortunately, there were no fatalities. It later transpired that the bomb had been placed beneath a passenger seat in the coach where the explosion occurred. Both trains were withdrawn from service.

IRA Mainland Campaign 1980s

For some reason, although the IRA continued their campaign in England during the 1980s they did not target the railway network. They concentrated their efforts mainly on military objectives, seaside holiday resorts, pub bombings, the leisure industry, and political targets. However, hoax bomb calls stating that explosive devices had been planted on railway stations did continue, disrupting many train services.

IRA Railway Targets – London – 1990s

On Monday, 18 February 1991, shortly before 5am, a bomb exploded at Paddington Station in London, causing extensive damage. Fortunately, there were no casualties. At 7.45am that morning, a second explosion occurred on the station concourse at Victoria Station, in which one man was killed and forty-three people, including women and children, were injured, some of them seriously and two critically. Both bombs had been placed in station litter bins. The IRA later claimed responsibility for the attacks. As a result of these two incidents, litter bins were withdrawn from railway stations throughout Britain to prevent a repeat of this new tactic being adopted by the IRA.

Commuter chaos hit London on Monday, 16 December 1991 when over half a million commuters were unable to get to work following an IRA explosion which caused damage to railway lines at Europe's busiest railway junction at Clapham. Warnings claiming to be from the IRA were telephoned to the programme *TV-AM*, at 6am, warning that bombs had been placed on 'all the mainline railway stations' in London. A short time later, an explosion occurred on the railway track at Clapham Junction in South London. The blast caused damage to the track, leaving a crater beneath. A train travelling on an adjacent track was rocked by the explosion but did not derail. There were no casualties in the Clapham Junction explosion but as a result of the bomb warning received by *TV-AM*, mainline stations at Waterloo, Victoria, Blackfriars, Charing Cross, London Bridge, Cannon Street, Paddington, Euston, St. Pancras, King's Cross, and Liverpool Street were all immediately closed and evacuated, together with all connecting Central London Underground Stations.

The capital was plunged into chaos on that day with thousands of rail passengers stranded, and although several IRA bombs did explode in London the same day, their targets had not included any mainline railway stations. No explosive devices were found at any of the railway stations, and they were all re-opened after several hours. Huge delays, cancellations and disruptions to train services continued for the rest of the day. A hoax bomb call had once again caused mayhem in London.

On Wednesday, 3 February 1993, the IRA struck the railway network once again in the capital. At 9am that morning, a telephone warning was received that a bomb had been planted on board the 9.05am train from London Victoria to Ramsgate. The train which consisted of twelve coaches was stopped at Kent House Station in South London and approximately eighty passengers were evacuated from it. Shortly afterwards, at 9.40am, an explosion occurred inside one of the passenger coaches of the train, blowing out windows and causing extensive damage. There were no casualties, but the train had to be taken out of service. The incident caused passenger delays as well as disrupting other services.

Shortly before 3.30pm the same day, another explosion occurred when the IRA targeted South Kensington Underground Station. An advance warning had been given, and the station had been evacuated when the bomb went off. Fortunately, the device had been planted in a disused lift shaft between the Piccadilly and District lines, and no serious damage was inflicted. There were no casualties.

British Soldiers Shot by IRA Gunmen

At about 5.50pm on Friday, 1 June 1990, three young men wearing civilian clothes were sitting on a seat on platform number two at Lichfield Railway Station in Staffordshire, waiting to catch a train to Birmingham. The men were army recruits from the Prince of Wales Division, Recruit Training Depot, Whittington Barracks, Lichfield, who were travelling home on weekend leave after completing twelve weeks of their initial training course at the barracks. The station was crowded with passengers.

Suddenly, two gunmen, both wearing balaclavas which covered their faces, appeared from amongst the waiting passengers, and screams were heard as six or seven shots rang out. The shots had been fired at the soldiers from point-blank range. There was panic on the station as the gunmen jumped from the platform and ran across the railway lines before climbing over the railway boundary fence and disappearing through a builder's yard.

One of the soldiers, William Roberts, aged 19 from Swansea was found slumped on a platform seat, having been shot dead. Alongside him was Robert Parkin a 20-year-old from Cheltenham. He was seriously injured with wounds to his head and shoulders. The third soldier was Neil Evans, aged 19 from Llanelli, South Wales. He had been shot in the right arm, but he was not seriously wounded.

Ambulances were quickly on the scene and the soldiers were rushed to Good Hope Hospital at Sutton Coldfield. A massive police operation quickly swung into action and a police helicopter scoured the area searching for the gunmen. The crime scene was sealed off whilst a forensic team worked late into the evening. Detectives from the Scotland Yard Terrorist Squad later teamed up with local detectives in the enquiry and an all-ports and airports warnings were circulated to the appropriate authorities. The IRA later claimed responsibility for the attack on the British soldiers, which remains unsolved.

IRA hostilities on the British Mainland came to an end in 1997 and a peace agreement was reached between the UK and Irish governments. Two pacts, which later became known as the Belfast or Good Friday Agreements were signed on 10 April 1998. The agreements have been upheld by both sides and lasting peace has prevailed ever since.

Chapter 7

Late Twentieth Century

Social Worker Murdered on a Train

On Wednesday, 20 March 1985, Mrs Janet Maddocks, aged 35, a social worker of King's Heath Birmingham, travelled by train to London. The purpose of her visit was twofold. She was meeting her husband who was in London, and she also had an appointment with a doctor in Harley Street who was treating her for a serious back injury which she had received in a car accident a few years earlier. After visiting the clinic in Harley Street, Janet, together with her husband Peter, visited the cinema and watched the film *A Passage to India*. The couple then went for a meal before going to Euston Railway Station in time for Janet to catch a train back to Birmingham shortly after 9pm. After kissing and waving her husband goodbye, Janet boarded the 9.02pm train to Birmingham, sitting in the second carriage from the front of the train.

The events which unfolded after the train left Euston are subject to some speculation, but it appears that a 16-year-old youth, Jack Roy, boarded the train when it stopped at Milton Keynes, and he sat in the same carriage as Janet Maddocks. Jack was travelling to his home in Glasgow. Sometime after the train left Milton Keynes, it appears that Jack Roy approached Janet Maddocks and made unwelcome advances towards her, which she rejected. Roy then forced himself upon her and started to pull down her tights and knickers with a view to raping her. Janet, it seems, continued to resist and fight off her attacker who then produced a knife and repeatedly stabbed her. She was knifed in the throat with such intensity that her spinal cord was severed. Evidence of further stabbing to her body was later found, including stab wounds to her groin which had occurred after her knickers and tights had been pulled down. Janet Maddocks was then dragged to a carriage door which was opened before she was thrown from the moving train like a rag doll, as it travelled through the Northamptonshire countryside.

When the train arrived at Birmingham New Street Station, officers of the British Transport Police were summoned after late-night passengers had alerted station staff to pools of blood inside the carriage. A British Transport Police scenes of crime officer, Jonathan Williams, was quickly on the scene, making a full examination of the carriage where the murder had taken place. He took samples of bloody footprints along the centre aisle of the coach, as well as blood samples and fingerprints from door-handles. He also took fingerprints from a toilet pan and wash basin in a lavatory at the end of the coach.

An extensive search of the railway track was carried out by British Transport Police officers and the bloodstained body of Janet Maddocks was eventually found on the railway line close to Brampton Bridge, just 3 miles north of Northampton. She was naked from the waist down except for her knickers and tights still around her ankles.

An extensive murder investigation was carried out which resulted in detectives visiting the home of Jack Roy, who lived in Shorebridge Street, Glasgow. He was arrested in connection with the wilful murder of Janet Maddocks. A search of his home was carried out in which a pair of his trainers were seized. It was later confirmed that the soles of the shoes matched the bloodstained shoeprints taken from the railway carriage where the murder had taken place. Bloodstained fingerprints found on door-handles inside the railway carriage and in the carriage toilet also belonged to Roy. Footprints which were found on the panties of Mrs Maddocks were also linked to the shoe soles recovered during the house search. Dr Michael Harris, a Home Office forensic scientist concluded that after stabbing Mrs Maddocks, Roy had trodden in her blood before treading onto her knickers, after they had been pulled down around her ankles.

During the house search, police carried out a search of Roy's bedroom where they recovered a knife which turned out to be the murder weapon. Dr Harris was later able to positively confirm by forensic tests that it was the knife used to stab Mrs Maddocks.

On Wednesday, 15 January 1986, Jack Roy appeared before Mr Justice Otton at the Birmingham Crown Court, charged with the wilful murder of Janet Maddocks. He pleaded not guilty. The defence claimed that Roy had no recollection of any of the events which took place that evening, after tripping with the hallucinatory drug LSD which he had taken earlier. On Tuesday, 21 January 1986, the trial of Jack Roy was concluded and Mr Rudi Narayan, defending, conceded that the evidence that his client had killed Janet Maddocks was 'overwhelming and irrefutable', but he argued that Roy, whom he described as a drifter, had been incapable of forming an intention to kill Mrs Maddocks because of his having taken LSD.

The jury, which consisted of seven men and five women, then retired to consider their verdict. After deliberating for four hours, the jury returned a verdict of guilty against Jack Roy on the charge of wilful murder. After hearing that Roy had previous convictions for attacking women, Mr Justice Otton ordered that he be detained during her Majesty's pleasure for the 'evil and callous' murder of a woman social worker on a late-night train. He went on to say that Jack Roy of Glasgow was a danger to women. He remarked:

> Having heard the evidence in this case, I am abundantly satisfied that this was an evil and callous killing. I have no doubt that on the evening you saw Mrs Maddocks alone in the railway carriage, you thought that she was an easy victim. Women you have attacked in the past had not resisted, but Mrs Maddock did resist, so you used your knife inflicting terrible wounds upon her. I have no doubt in my mind that what you did was deliberate, and I am satisfied that you are a danger to women.

Slightly-built Roy showed no emotion as he was led from the dock. After being incarcerated for not less than twenty years, Jack Roy was released on licence at the age of 36 in 2005 and went to live at an address in Edinburgh.

Murder and Rape in the Capital

During the 1980s, police began to suspect that not just one, but two serial rapists were at large in London. Tensions mounted as the numbers of these appalling crimes increased, all of which it seemed were being committed upon or in the vicinity of the railway network. As a result, the unknown perpetrators of these crimes became referred to as the 'Railway Rapists'.

In July 1982, an un-named woman was brutally attacked and raped by two men during the hours of darkness at an isolated spot in the vicinity of Hamstead Heath Railway Station in North-London. During the attack, one of her assailants threatened her with a knife. Similar attacks, involving either one or two attackers, took place over the next twelve months, in both north and south London, with few or no clues as to the identity of the offenders. As the number of attacks increased, a pattern did start to emerge which caused some alarm for the detectives involved in these investigations. Whilst the victims of the attacks being carried out in North London were reporting two men as being the perpetrators, victims of the attacks in South London, all reported that the offender was one man acting alone. Police now had to face the reality that the rapes committed in North London were committed by different individuals to the ones being committed in South London. This meant that not just two rapists were at large, but there were in fact, three serial rapists operating in London.

A breakthrough came in July 1984, when Alan Pearey, aged 35, of Ferrier Estate, Kidbrooke, South East London was identified by police from an artist's portrait impression of a suspect, produced from a description given by a railway rape victim. Pearey was arrested and subsequently charged with several offences of rape committed either upon or near the railway in South London. He was remanded in custody whilst awaiting trial at the Old Bailey.

On Tuesday, 15 January 1985, Alan Pearey appeared before Mr Justice Popplewell. The prosecutor was Graham Boal QC, and Anthony Glass QC represented Pearey. The defendant faced six charges of rape, one charge of assaulting a 14-year-old schoolgirl and three other indecent assaults on females over a period spanning from April 1983 to July 1984. Pearey pleaded guilty to all the charges.

Graham Boal QC told the court that for sixteen months, in the Bexley and Welling areas of South London, women walked and travelled in fear as ten women fell victim to Pearey. They were attacked either in train carriages whilst travelling to and from Charing Cross, or as they walked in lonely spots. One of the victims was a 16-year-old schoolgirl who was raped near Falconwood Railway Station. Although unemployed at the time of his arrest, Pearey had spent his working life on the railway in South-London, first as a porter, then as a trainee signalman, using his knowledge of the South London rail network when seeking his rape victims.

Sentencing Pearey, Judge Popplewell told him that the only mitigation in his favour was his plea of guilty. He went on to say, 'You terrified and humiliated these victims. I think you are a dangerous man to be left at large. The public must be protected from men like you and I propose to pass the maximum sentence in law.' Although Pearey had shown some remorse for the crimes he had committed, he stared at his feet and showed no emotion as he was sentenced to serve six life sentences for rapes and sexual attacks. After his conviction, detectives focussed their attention to the railway rapes which were still being committed in North London, usually by two men.

The North London railway rapes had started in earnest in 1982, and no less than thirty similar offences occurred over the next three years. The modus operandi in each case was similar. The assailants were both men in their mid-twenties The offences occurred in isolated places on or near the railway in North London, during the hours of darkness. The victims usually had their hands bound with string and sometimes a knife was used to threaten the victim before a brutal rape took place. On one occasion in 1985, three different women were attacked and raped by two men in Hendon on the same night.

At that time (1985), rapid improvements in DNA technology had enabled it to be used for the first time to assist in solving crimes such as rape and murder, and although still in its infancy, police were optimistic that this new development in forensics had the potential to contribute towards solving these cases. In the meantime, as the new year approached, the actions of the railway rapists were about to turn even more sinister.

On Sunday, 29 December 1985, Alison Day aged 19, travelled by train on the North London railway line to Hackney Wick Railway Station in East London where she had arranged to meet her boyfriend. He worked for a printing company near the station, and she frequently visited him when he was working an evening shift to keep him company. She alighted from the train after dark and as she left the station, two men attacked her. She was dragged to some waste ground nearby where both men brutally raped her. Day then somehow managed to escape but was chased onto a nearby railway bridge from where she was either thrown, pushed, or jumped into a canal below.

Having landed in the canal, Day swam to the side as the two men scrambled down the railway embankment from the bridge towards her. The men pulled her from the water onto the canal towpath. There, they ripped off her blouse and tore it into three pieces. One piece was placed over her mouth to gag her and prevent her screaming. Her hands were tied by another piece to restrain her, and the third piece was then placed around her neck and used to strangle her to death. Her body was then carried a short distance to the bank of the adjacent river Lea where stones were placed in her pockets to weigh her down before she was dumped into the river, sinking beneath the murky waters. The body of Alison Day remained in the river Lea for two weeks before it was discovered, and a murder investigation named 'Operation LEA' was set up to investigate it. The 'railway rapists' were then renamed the 'railway killers'.

On 17 April 1986, a Dutch schoolgirl, Maartje Tamboezer, aged 15, left her home at Horsley in Surrey and rode her bicycle to a local shop to buy some sweets. As she rode along an isolated footpath near Horsley Railway Station, she was unaware that two men were watching her. After visiting the shop, she returned along the pathway and the two men tied a length of fishing line across the path, causing her to fall off her bicycle. Maartje was dragged into some nearby woods where she was brutally raped and then murdered after being struck on the head with a large stone to render her unconscious, before being strangled. The men set fire to her body to destroy any evidence, before leaving the scene. A murder investigation called 'Operation Bluebell' was set up by the Surrey Constabulary. Due to the geographical location of this murder, there was no suggestion that it was linked to the murder of Alison Day in North London during the initial stages of this investigation.

Meanwhile, Detective Superintendent Charles Farquhar of the Metropolitan Police, who had been put in charge of the investigation involving the murder of Alison Day, did find evidence which suggested that her murder had been committed by the same men who had been carrying out the North London railway rapes. Later, Superintendent Farquar also managed to discover a link between the murder of Alison Day in Hackney and that of Maartje Tamboezer in Horsley. As a result of this breakthrough, the two murders became a joint murder enquiry involving three separate police forces, namely the Metropolitan Police, the Surrey Constabulary, and the British Transport Police, who were responsible for policing the railways.

On 18 May 1986, Anne Locke, aged 29, a secretary employed by London Weekend Television, left work at 8.30pm to commute to her home at Brookmans Park, a village in Hertfordshire, approximately forty minutes journey time by train from King's Cross. After arriving at her destination after dark, she alighted from the train and went to pick up her bike from outside the station when two men grabbed her. Anne was forced to walk alongside the railway line to an isolated field where her stockings were removed. One stocking was stuffed into her mouth and the other was used to strangle her after she had been raped. An attempt was made to burn her body before it was left lying in the undergrowth, where it remained for almost two months before the decomposed remains were discovered. The local police set up a murder enquiry and when links were found with the murders of Alison Day and Maartje Tamboezer, the Hertfordshire Constabulary became the fourth police force to become a part of the multi-force murder enquiry which was then renamed 'Operation Trinity' to jointly investigate all three railway murders.

In November 1986 a man named John Francis Duffy, aged 28, a former railway carpenter, was arrested by police whilst pursuing a woman through a secluded park in London during the hours of darkness. As a result of an interview, his description, and enquiries into his background, he became a suspect in connection with the railway rapes and murders being investigated. Enquires showed that Duffy was already known to police, after having been previously arrested and charged with the rape of his estranged wife, an offence for which he was never convicted. A search was carried out at an address where he lived with his parents, and possible evidence linking him to the murder of Maartje Tamboezer was found.

Duffy, who matched several of the criminal profiles compiled during the murder investigations, was questioned at great length and although many victims failed to identify him, a total of seven rape victims did pick him out from identity parades as being their attacker. Duffy failed to co-operate with police throughout the enquiry, and he strenuously denied any involvement in any of the murders or the rapes that had occurred. He was questioned at great length about having an accomplice but again he refused to co-operate and denied all knowledge of accomplices or indeed the crimes themselves. Having been picked out of identity parades by seven different rape victims, there was ample evidence against him, and John Duffy was later charged with offences of murder and rape. He was remanded in custody.

On Tuesday, 12 January 1988, John Francis Duffy, aged twenty-nine, a former railway worker, appeared before Mr Justice Farquarson at the Old Bailey charged with three counts of the wilful murder of Alison Day, Maartje Tamboezer and Anne Locke. In addition, he was further charged with seven counts of rape, one of indecency, one malicious wounding and two assaults.

He pleaded not guilty on all fourteen charges. The prosecution was conducted by Mr Anthony Hooper QC, assisted by Mr Laurence Lock and the defendant was represented by Mr David Farrington.

Opening the case for the prosecution, Hooper stressed that it was the evidence relating to the murder of Maartje Tamboezer that was crucial to the entire case. Maartje, who attended a Dutch School on the American Community School Campus between Cobham and Esher, disappeared on the way to the village shop near her home in East Horsley.

On 17 April 1986 she had set off on her bicycle along the footpath bordering the railway line. The Dutch-born schoolgirl was forced to stop, said Mr Hooper, because Mr Duffy has stretched a piece of nylon gut across the path. There, the attacker forced her to walk into a field. Her shoes were covered in mud. Her bicycle was left against a tree in the corner of the field, and she was forced to walk into the middle of a nearby wood. She was raped and knocked unconscious with severe head injuries. Her wrists were tied behind her back, incurring fractures to her thumbs. Maartje was strangled with her own narrow leather belt using a tourniquet technique with a piece of wood, but the belt broke under the pressure of the leverage, so she was finally strangled with her own scarf.

Mr Hooper claimed that Duffy then set fire to her body. Some Swan Vestas matches were recovered from the scene of the murder together with some partially burned tissue paper. The body of Maartje was found the next morning. Police later found a box of Swan Vestas matches inside Duffy's house. Also stuffed into the matchbox (presumably to start a fire) was some tissue paper identical to the piece recovered from the crime scene at

Horsley. All three murder victims had been strangled in the same manner, by a unique and most extraordinary method involving a loop of clothing around the neck, tightened like a tourniquet with a piece of wood. Also in his opening remarks, Mr Hooper told the jury that seven different rape victims had all picked out Duffy from identity parades.

On Friday, 27 April 1988, following a six-week trial at the Central Criminal Court in London, the jury returned to deliver a verdict against John Francis Duffy. After pleading not guilty to fourteen charges, the verdict delivered by the jury was as follows: murder of Alison Day – guilty; murder of Maartje Tamboezer – guilty; murder of Anne Locke – not guilty due to insufficient evidence.

Duffy was also convicted on four counts of rape. The remaining charges were dismissed due to lack of evidence.

In passing sentence, Mr Justice Farquarson told Duffy that in respect of the murders of Alison Day and Maartje Tamboezer, 'The wickedness and beastliness of the murders committed on those two very young girls hardly bears description.' He branded the 5ft 4in tall former British Rail carpenter a 'predatory animal'.

Judge Farquarson then sentenced Duffy to serve seven separate life sentences, and he recommended that he serve at least thirty years. Although police did strongly believe that Duffy was also responsible for the murder of Ann Locke, there was insufficient evidence, in part due to the lack of forensic evidence resulting from the badly decomposed state of her remains.

Since the early 1980s, police had been quite certain that most of the railway rapes committed in North London involved two men. After his arrest, John Duffy was questioned at great length about numerous unsolved rapes and about having an accomplice. He denied all the offences put to him, and by doing so denied the existence of an accomplice. He also refused to answer any questions about any friends or former friends or acquaintances that he had known over the years.

In the meantime, however, police did produce a name of someone who they believed may have been a partner in crime with Duffy. They strongly suspected that this person participated in rapes (and later the murders) which they attributed to Duffy. The person in question was a former school friend of his called David Mulcahy; they were about same age, and both boys were born in Ireland. David Mulcahy had been arrested by police on suspicion of murder and rape, whilst John Duffy was being remanded in custody. Mulcahy however refused to speak to police, and there was no forensic evidence to connect him to any of the crimes. He was subsequently released due to lack of evidence.

Duffy first met Mulcahy when they became pupils together in Haverstock Secondary School at Chalk Farm in North London. Duffy, who was short in stature, was an aggressive individual but was often bullied because of his size and he did not mix with other boys. Mulcahy was to some extent a misfit and very much a loner in school, but after a while the boys became friends. As time passed, an inseparable friendship developed between the two boys, and it transpired that both possessed sadistic tendencies. They both enjoyed inflicting pain on helpless animals, although it seemed that Mulcahy was without doubt the more violent and aggressive of the two and was even given the nickname 'Crazy Davey'. Duffy and Mulcahy spent their teen years together and visited places such as Hamstead Heath where they would terrorise young children and spy on courting couples. During the mid-1970s Duffy and Mulcahy both married their respective girlfriends. Mulcahy was employed as a plasterer and Duffy became a carpenter with British Rail where he gained extensive knowledge about the North London railway network and railway stations which he would later use to his advantage when seeking rape victims.

In the early 1980s, Duffy and Mulcahy made a pact which resulted in them trawling the railways of North London seeking vulnerable young women who they could attack. It is believed that their first rape victim was a 21-year-old woman who was brutally raped in the Kilburn area of London whilst walking home after dark carrying a teddy bear. Duffy and Mulcahy grabbed hold of her and said, 'Don't worry, all we want is your teddy.' A plaster was put over her mouth and she was threatened with a knife before being bundled over a wall and viciously raped by Mulcahy, then raped again by Duffy.

In 1997, some nine years after his convictions for murder and rape, John Francis Duffy started receiving psychiatric counselling from Dr Jenny Cutler whilst serving his sentence at Whitemoor Prison in Cambridgeshire. During a conversation with Dr Cutler, he mentioned that when he committed the murders and rapes, he was not acting alone. This was the first tangible evidence that Duffy had an accomplice whilst committing his crimes. The matter was brought to the attention of police who later re-interviewed Duffy in prison. The interviews which took place in the prison were recorded on tape.

During the interviews, Duffy reconsidered his story and admitted having committed the murders with which he was charged, including the murder of Anne Locke for which he had been acquitted. He also admitted that David Mulcahy had been his accomplice all along and he too had taken part in each of the three murders. He went on to admit numerous other unsolved cases of rape, the majority of which, he said, were committed in company with Mulcahy. Despite these new admissions, police were unable to charge Duffy with the murder of Anne Locke as he had already been acquitted of her murder (double jeopardy), but he was later charged with raping her. In total, John Francis Duffy was charged with a further seventeen offences of rape and conspiracy to rape, which he said were committed in company with David Mulcahy.

In March 1999, Duffy again appeared before the Old Bailey where he pleaded guilty to seventeen further charges of rape and conspiracy to rape. The case was adjourned and Duffy was finally sentenced on 2 February 2001 when, although already serving a full life sentence, he was sentenced to serve an additional twelve years on each of the seven rape charges. It is highly unlikely that he will ever be released from prison.

Following the admissions made in prison by Duffy that David Mulcahy had been involved in three murders and numerous rapes, detectives focussed their attention on Mulcahy with a view to bringing him to justice. Although Duffy had given a written statement to police implicating Mulcahy, and offered to give evidence against him in court, this was insufficient to prefer charges against him, as the law clearly states that evidence given by an accomplice must be corroborated.

Over a decade had passed since David Mulcahy had been arrested by police on suspicion of being involved with John Duffy in connection with incidents involving murder and rape. On that occasion, Mulcahy had to be released without charge due to lack of evidence, although detectives carrying out those investigations were optimistic that the introduction of a new form of forensic science involving DNA would eventually play a key role in solving the cases. That prediction was about to be put to the test.

Between the mid-1980s and the late 1990s, advancements in DNA technology for solving crimes had grown in leaps and bounds. Forensic experts carried out a meticulous examination of exhibits and evidence which had been placed into storage after the original investigations. They had some amazing success and at last they were able to prove without any doubt that Mulcahy was involved in the murders and rapes of many of the victims. This new DNA evidence, together with the latest admissions made by Duffy, was ample evidence to secure convictions against Mulcahy for offences of murder and rape.

In February 1999, David Mulcahy was arrested at his home and a search of the premises revealed further evidence connecting him to the crimes. He was later charged with three offences of murder and several rapes, before being remanded in custody.

In September 2000, he appeared before Judge Michael Hyam at the Old Bailey, charged with the following offences: the murders of Alison Day, Maartje Tamboezer and Anne Locke; seven offences of rape; and five offences of conspiracy to rape.

Mulcahy pleaded not guilty to all fifteen charges.

John Duffy was one of the witnesses called by the prosecution to give evidence, and he testified against his former friend. At the conclusion of the trial, the jury returned a verdict of guilty in respect of all fifteen charges.

Judge Hyam told Mulcahy, 'The murders were a sadistic killing. I have no doubt that you deprived gratification from the act of killing.' He went on to say that Mulcahy became a different person. He was excited by dominance and thrived on the total control it gave him.

Judge Hyam then passed the following sentences upon Mulcahy. Three life sentences for the murders of Day, Tamboezer and Locke. Twenty-four years imprisonment for each of the seven counts of rape (concurrent). Eighteen years imprisonment for each of the five counts of conspiring to rape (concurrent). As with the case of Duffy, his partner in crime, Mulcahy is unlikely to ever be released from prison.

Woman Murdered on a Train

Deborah Ann Linsley was born in October 1961 and was brought up in Bromley, Kent where she lived with her parents until she moved to Edinburgh in 1987 to work as a hotel manager. In the spring of 1988, Deborah had the opportunity to attend a hotel management course in London, so she returned to Bromley to stay with her parents from where she could commute into London daily by train for the duration of the course.

On the afternoon of Wednesday, 23 March 1988, 26-year-old Deborah was given a lift by car to Petts Wood Railway Station in Bromley by her brother Gordon, who dropped her off in time to catch the 2.15pm train to London Victoria. Deborah boarded the train and sat in a second-class compartment. It is not known whether or not there were any other occupants in the compartment when she boarded.

The train in question was a local slow stopping train from Orpington, which after leaving Petts Wood called at Bickley, Bromley South, Shortlands, Beckenham, Kent House, Penge, Sydenham Hill, West Dulwich, Herne Hill, Brixton and London Victoria, where it was due to arrive at 2.50pm, a journey time of just 35 minutes.

The train arrived at Victoria Station on time, and about seventy passengers alighted from it. A railway member of staff then walked along the length of the train, which was standard procedure, to ensure that all passengers had alighted from the train, as well as checking that the doors were closed. It was whilst checking the train, that a member of staff found the bloodstained body of Deborah Linsley lying on the floor of the compartment. Both the floor and the compartment seats were covered in blood.

It was later established that Deborah had been viciously attacked and stabbed to death. She sustained eleven stab wounds to the face, neck, and abdomen and five stab wounds to the heart, any one of which could have caused her death. It was believed that the ferocious and savage stabbing was carried out by a person using a knife with a blade measurement of between 5 and 8 inches. The murder weapon was never found.

A postmortem was later carried out, followed by an inquest on 16 November, where the jury returned a verdict of unlawful killing. Despite a lengthy murder investigation being carried out, no witnesses to the attack ever came forward. DNA samples taken at the crime scene have never been matched to anyone in the DNA database. Although there was evidence that Deborah struggled to fight off her attacker, which was supported by wounds on her hands where she had tried to defend herself, there was no evidence of any sexual interference with the victim, or any indication that she had been robbed. Sadly, the case remains unsolved.

The funeral of Deborah Linsley took place at the Holy Trinity Church in Bromley on 22 April 1988. She was buried in a nearby cemetery wearing a bridesmaid's dress which she was due to have worn at her brother's forthcoming wedding.

Murdered on a Footpath in Rural Surrey

At approximately 7.30pm on Wednesday, 5 March 1992, Mrs Manzula Amlani, aged 43, an insurance clerk, alighted from a train at Bagshot Railway Station in Surrey. She was returning home after attending a training course in connection with her work.

Mrs Amlani left the station and began walking along a railway footpath when suddenly she was approached by a young man who was brandishing a kitchen knife. The man threatened Mrs Amlani before brutally raping her. The man then, without warning, carried out a frenzied attack by stabbing Mrs Amlani six times, inflicting severe wounds to her face, chest, back and arms, before finally slashing her across the throat.

The attacker then fled the scene, leaving the victim lying on the footpath in a pool of blood where she died from shock and severe loss of blood.

A murder enquiry was conducted by police which subsequently resulted in the arrest of Ian Russell, aged 22, a local unemployed man living in Bagshot with his girlfriend, Margaret McAvoy, and her 13-year-old son. Russell was later charged with the rape and murder of Mrs Amlani. He was remanded in custody before appearing at the local Magistrate's Court where he was committed to stand trial at the Old Bailey.

On Monday, 1 February 1993, Ian Russell appeared before the Central Criminal Court charged with the rape and murder of Mrs Manzula Amlani. Russell pleaded 'not guilty' on both counts.

Mr John Nutting QC, prosecuting, outlined the circumstances of the case, and told the court that Mrs Amlani moved from Kenya to England in 1986 and lived alone in the village of Bagshot. She was a quiet individual who was well liked by her neighbours.

Nutting continued by telling the court that on the day of the murder, the defendant Russell had been drinking and smoking cannabis with a friend before walking to the local railway station. He was in possession of a kitchen knife which, it was later established, had been bought by his girlfriend for use in the kitchen at home. Upon arrival at the station, he saw Mrs Amlani get off the train and walk along the railway footpath which was otherwise deserted. Russell followed her onto the footpath and carried out the vicious attack. Following the rape and brutal murder of Mrs Amlani, Russell fled the scene and returned to his home leaving his victim for dead.

A postmortem later confirmed that the extent of the wounds inflicted were the cause of death, and it also revealed that the victim had been raped.

Mr Nutting went on to say that when Russell arrived home after the murder, he spent the evening drinking champagne and smoking cannabis. The following morning, he returned to the scene of the crime where blood stains from the victim were still visible on the footpath. He again returned to his home where he smoked more cannabis.

Evidence from both Margaret McAvoy, Russell's girlfriend, and her son was given that on the day following the murder Russell, who was under the influence of the cannabis which he was smoking, re-enacted the stabbing of a murder victim by poking McAvoy's teenage son twice in the chest with his thumb before making a cutting movement with his hand across his throat.

The prosecution also informed the court that when the murder was carried out, Russell had been wearing a pair of football goalkeeper's gloves. The gloves were later found near the scene of the crime, along with the murder weapon. The gloves bore blood stains from the victim as well as traces of blood belonging to Russell himself, which matched a gash on his hand which it appeared he had sustained whilst carrying out the attack. Traces of blood were also found in the hall, stairway, and bathroom of the house where Russell was living.

The trial of Ian Russell lasted for two weeks and the evidence against him was overwhelming. The jury found him guilty on both counts. Ian

Russell was sentenced to life imprisonment for the wilful murder of Manzula Amlani and sentenced to serve ten years (concurrent) for the offence of rape.

The James Bulger Murder

James Patrick Bulger was born at Kirkby in Merseyside on 16 March 1990. On Friday, 12 February 1993, James, who was almost 3 years old, had been taken by his mother Denise to the Strand shopping precinct in Bootle near Liverpool. At about 3.40pm that afternoon, Denise went into Tyms butchers' shop, accompanied by James who was holding her hand. Denise let go of his hand to buy some meat and when she turned around a few moments later, there was no sign of James. Denise ran out of the shop, but James had completely disappeared. A search was made of the surrounding area by security staff but there was no sign of the little boy. Police were summoned and a major search was launched whilst police were comforting his distraught mother. A description of James, who was wearing a blue anorak with a hood, trainers and silver coloured tracksuit trousers, was circulated throughout the district.

The shopping precinct closed at 5.30pm and there was still no sign of the missing child, so police and security staff spent the evening searching through CCTV footage of the shopping precinct and surrounding areas. Their efforts were rewarded when CCTV footage showed James in the presence of two young boys walking away from the precinct towards the Leeds and Liverpool Canal. One of the boys was holding James by the hand. It appeared that the two boys had abducted James. Despite their best efforts, the police searches revealed nothing as to the whereabouts of James who remained missing for two days.

On Sunday, 14 February police officers who were still searching for James made a gruesome discovery when they found his battered body lying on a railway line on top of an embankment near Walton Lane in Liverpool. The location was about 2.5 miles from where he was abducted. A postmortem later revealed that had been stamped upon and kicked to death. There were twenty-two bruises, and grazes to his face and a further twenty wounds on his body. It was established that an iron bar had been dropped several times on the toddler's head causing ten separate fractures to his skull. The boy had been stoned by railway ballast and bricks had been thrown at him. Two batteries had been stuffed into his mouth and down the back of his throat. James had then been laid across the railway track in a feeble attempt to make his death look like an accident. Detective Inspector Albert Kirkby, who led the murder enquiry suspected that this horrific murder may have been carried out by two young boys.

Two 10-year-olds, Robert Thompson and Jon Venables were subsequently arrested in connection with the abduction and murder of James Bulger. They both appeared before South Sefton Magistrates' Court in Bootle on 22 February 1993. Due to their age, they were not publicly identified but referred to as boy A and boy B. They were both committed to stand trial at Liverpool Crown Court. The court was packed and a crowd of over 300 people gathered outside the court. Later, rioting broke out as the prison van sped away carrying the two prisoners. The court case quickly made sensational news headlines nationwide and was widely reported throughout the media where it was publicised as one of the most shocking crimes ever committed in British history.

On 1 November 1993, the trial of Robert Thompson and Jon Venables commenced at Preston Crown Court, the case having been transferred there from Liverpool due to public anger and the fear of more rioting taking place if the case was heard in Liverpool. Both boys pleaded not guilty to the charges of abduction and wilful murder. The trial judge was Mr Justice Morland. Again, an injunction was made, preventing the press from releasing the names and details of the two defendants.

The court was told that at about 12.30pm on 12 February 1993, a mere three hours before James Bulger was abducted, the accused had tried to abduct another little boy from his mother in the same shopping precinct. Whilst paying for her shopping, her son disappeared so she ran outside the shop and saw the two boys walking away, beckoning her son to follow them. She screamed and shouted her son's name who then returned to her. After their arrest for the James Bulger murder, the boys did admit to the earlier abduction attempt, and during a police interview, they told police that they intended to find a young child and throw him into the path of a bus or taxi on the road outside the shopping precinct and make it look like an accident.

During the trial, a total of thirty-eight witnesses gave evidence of seeing James Bulger with the two boys on his 2.5 mile journey from the shopping precinct to the railway line where he was murdered. Each witness gave evidence of what they saw and some of the witnesses stated that they had spoken to the boys, due to concerns about the toddler. The boys said the James was their young brother. All these witnesses blamed themselves for not interfering or getting involved. Forensic scientist Graham Jackson also gave evidence that blood samples taken from James Bulger matched a bloodstain on a shoe belonging to boy B. There was only one in a billion chance of it being an error.

Other forensic scientists and experts also gave similar evidence which connected various different items of clothing and footwear from both boys A and B to the body of James Bulger. The trial which lasted over three-weeks dominated the headlines in British newspapers, television, and other forms of the media, until on 24 November the jury retired to consider their verdicts. After deliberating for six hours the jury returned a verdict of guilty against both boys for the abduction and wilful murder of James Bulger.

The injunction preventing the press from releasing details of the two boys was lifted and the two boys were sentenced by the Judge, Mr Justice Morland. Robert Thompson and Jon Venables were given life sentences, and the Judge recommended that they serve a minimum sentence of eight years.

On 22 June 2001, having served their eight years, Thompson and Venables were released on life licence. They were both given new identities and moved to different parts of the country.

Concrete Blocks Cause Fatal Train Crash

At 10.45pm on Saturday, 25 June 1994, a three-coach, electric powered, multiple unit passenger train departed Wemyss Bay Railway Station on the Firth of Clyde, bound for Glasgow Central Station. At about 11pm, as the train was passing through Dumfrocher near Greenock on a stretch of single-track railway line, the train came into contact with some concrete blocks which had been deliberately placed across the railway lines by vandals. The train, which was travelling at approximately 50mph, left the track and smashed into an over-bridge near Peat Road Greenock before coming to a halt. The driver's cab of the train was crushed by the impact, and the train driver, Arthur McKee, aged 35, of Baillieston, Glasgow was crushed to death and died almost instantly. His wife had been waiting for him at Glasgow Central Station to give him a lift home after he had finished his shift.

A 21-year-old passenger, Alan Nicol, a student, of Blairmore Road. Greenock who was in the front coach of the train, was also killed after being hurled through a carriage door which was ripped off its hinges by the impact. He had been standing by the door, waiting to alight from the train at Greenock. His body was found on a railway embankment alongside the wreckage of the train. Several other passengers on the train were also injured. The guard, Brian McGuire, aged 26, had a very lucky escape. He would normally have been in the front cab with the driver when the accident occurred, but after checking tickets, he was engaged in a conversation with one of the passengers in the middle coach of the train.

Emergency services attended the scene and police later confirmed that the derailment had been caused by some 3ft long reinforced concrete cable-trough covers having been placed across the railway lines. The covers had been deliberately removed from the concrete troughs which run alongside the railway lines to carry signalling cables. Police immediately treated the deaths as murder and an investigation got underway.

On Tuesday, 28 June, just three days after the crash, detectives arrested two 17-year-old youths, Gary Dougan of Prospecthill Street, Greenock, and Craig Houston of Holefarm Road, Greenock, after other witnesses had come forward, placing them at the scene of the crime. When interviewed later, Gary Dougan told detectives that on the night in question he had been drinking beer with Houston, and they went to the road bridge crossing the railway with their girlfriends. The two youths wanted to go to the toilet, so they walked down the railway embankment and onto the railway track to relieve themselves. The girlfriends stayed on top of the bridge. He said that Houston smashed a beer bottle on the track before picking up some concrete trough covers and putting them across the railway lines. He went on to tell detectives that he told Houston to stop being so stupid and put the covers back because they could cause an accident. He said that Houston told him, 'Don't be so daft, the train will go right through them.' Dougan then told detectives that he then walked back up the embankment to join the girls on the bridge, and left Houston on the railway line. He denied placing anything on the track himself. He also said that he did not assist Houston to remove the duct covers from the cable-troughs and was not involved in any way whatsoever. Douglas then made a written statement to police in the presence of his lawyer.

When Craig Houston was later interviewed in the presence of his lawyer, the interview was recorded on tape. He denied the events as outlined by Dougan and said that Dougan must have placed the concrete trough covers across the railway lines, because he was not involved. He admitted on tape that he was on the railway track with Dougan before going back on his own to the bridge to join their girlfriends. He said, 'We stood on the top of the bridge for a while, maybe four or five minutes waiting for Gary to come up. Gary eventually came running up but never said anything about placing concrete covers on the track.' He went on to say that later that night, friends told him there had been a train crash, and that was the first time he knew about it.

Both youths were later charged with the murders of train driver Arthur McKee and student Alan Nicol. The trial subsequently took place at Glasgow High Court before Lord Murray and both youths pleaded not guilty.

On 22 December 1994, the trial was concluded. Gary Dougan and Craig Houston were both acquitted of wilful murder, but both were found guilty of culpable homicide (Scottish law equivalent of manslaughter). Lord Murray sentenced both defendants to serve a term of fifteen years imprisonment.

Body Remains Found in Disused Railway Hut

On Thursday, 19 January 1995, Mrs Yvette Wilson, aged 27 from Ayrshire in Scotland went to catch a train from her local railway station, West Kilbride. The station itself was a quiet village station which was unmanned. As she stood on the deserted platform waiting for her train to arrive, she was approached by a 25-year-old man, Edward Mullen, who engaged in a conversation with her.

Shortly afterwards, Mullen made advances towards her and tried to kiss her. Mrs Wilson pushed Mullen away and told him to leave her alone.

Mullen again grabbed hold of Mrs Wilson, and a struggle broke out as she tried to fight off his advances. Mullen then dragged Mrs Wilson along the station platform to a nearby disused wooden railway hut. He threw her inside where he continued to molest her. Mrs Wilson still resisted, but Mullen overpowered her and beat her until she was unconscious. Mullen then set fire to the hut whilst the body of Mrs Wilson was still inside.

Two days later, following a report from railway officials of suspected arson to the disused railway hut at West Kilbride Station, officers of the British Transport Police visited the site and examined the remains of the partially burned-out hut. Upon entering the hut, they came across the remains of a charred body. The head and upper part of the body was so badly burned that identification was impossible.

The body was later identified as a result of DNA tests being carried out, as well as the identification of items of jewellery recovered from the body. A fingerprint, found on the door of the shed, which had not been destroyed in the blaze, was later positively identified as belonging to Edward Mullen.

Edward Mullen was subsequently arrested for the wilful murder of Yvette Wilson and when interviewed by police, he began sobbing and confessed to the crime.

On Thursday, 18 May, Edward Mullen appeared before Kilmarnock High Court where he pleaded guilty to the wilful murder of Yvette Wilson. After the facts had been outlined, the court was told that in January, when the offence took place, Mullen had just been freed from prison after serving a five-year sentence for assaulting a female with intent to rape her.

After sentencing Mullen to life imprisonment for the murder of Yvette Wison, the judge, Lord Osborne, told Mullen that he should serve at least fifteen years.

Railway Signalman Stabbed Works Colleague

On Wednesday, 2 August 1995, two railwaymen who were working a night shift at Middlesborough in North Yorkshire were sitting in a cabin chatting together whilst having a tea break. Suddenly, an argument broke out between the two men and Douglas Vinter, a 25-year-old railway signalman from Coppice Road, Middlesborough, pulled out a knife and stabbed Carl Edon, his 22-year-old colleague to death. Vinter returned to his duties as if nothing had happened and the body of Edon was not discovered until the following day.

Upon discovery of the body, a murder investigation was launched, and Douglas Vinter was subsequently arrested by police and charged with the wilful murder of Carl Edon. Vinter appeared before Teeside Magistrates Court on 11 August where he was remanded in custody to stand trial in the Crown Court.

In May 1996, Vinter appeared in Teeside Crown Court where he pleaded guilty to the wilful murder of a former colleague Carl Edon. He was sentenced to life imprisonment and the judge recommended that he serve a minimum of ten years behind bars.

Vinter was released from prison in 1996 and moved to Teesside. The following year, he married Annie White, but their marriage was a stormy one. Vinter was a very well-built, strong and powerful man, who stood 6ft 7ins tall. He practised bodybuilding in his spare time. He was also a bully with a quick temper who had beaten his wife on at least two previous occasions. His wife soon realised that her marriage to Vinter had been a mistake, so she decided to leave him. When Annie informed Douglas that their marriage was over, he started to drink alcohol and take drugs before going berserk. He then picked up a kitchen knife and repeatedly stabbed his wife before strangling her to death.

On 21 April 2008, Vinter again appeared before Teesside Crown Court where he pleaded guilty to murdering his wife. He was again sentenced to life imprisonment and the judge recommended on this occasion, that he should never be released from prison.

In November 2014, whilst incarcerated in Milton Keynes Prison, Vinter had an altercation with another inmate, convicted murderer Lee Newell. In a fit of rage, Vintner repeatedly kicked Newell about the head and body before being restrained by prison officers.

One prison officer later said that the injuries sustained by Newell were the worst he had ever seen in his twenty-one years as a prison officer. Newell received brain injuries and was blinded in one eye as a result of the beating. Vinter told a prison officer, 'That's what you get when you mess me about.' Vinter was subsequently charged with the attempted murder of Lee Newell. The case was heard at Luton Crown Court and part way through the trial, Vinter changed his plea from not guilty to guilty. He was given a further life sentence which means that he is now serving whole-life sentences and will never be released from prison.

Woman's Body Dumped on Railway Line

Not long after daybreak on Tuesday, 12 December 1995, the naked dismembered body of a woman was discovered on a railway line just outside the village of Blisworth, approximately six-miles from Northampton. She had been run over by a freight train and possibly struck by a second train. Police officers attended the scene, and a murder investigation was soon underway.

Facial recognition of the body was not possible due to its mutilated state, but fingerprints taken from the victim identified her as being Daniella White, a 28-year-old prostitute and drug addict who lived in Edith Street, Northampton. A postmortem was later conducted, but due to the extent of mutilations and injuries to all parts of the body caused by the passing trains, it was not possible to establish a cause of death.

Police strongly suspected that Daniella had been murdered at another location by someone who had used her services as a prostitute. The body was then taken and placed on the railway line during the hours of darkness, with the sole intention that her body would be badly mangled by passing trains to destroy any evidence of the murder. Accordingly, the murder investigation focussed upon sex workers and their clients in the Northampton area.

Enquiries revealed that Daniella was last seen alive, and plying her trade at 12.45am, about seven hours before her body was discovered. She was seen at Beaumont Court, in Northampton. This was a welcome breakthrough for the police during their investigation.

A major murder hunt for the killer of Daniella White followed. It was carried out by a team of fifty police officers led by Detective Chief Inspector Dave Armiger. More than 700 people were interviewed, which included many of her former clients. Over 400 statements were taken, and over 200 telephone calls were received by murder squad detectives hunting the killer.

Police even broke with tradition by offering a £5,000 reward for information leading to the apprehension and conviction of the vice-girl's killer.

The investigation continued relentlessly for over a year, until in February 1997, Philip Anthony McKenna, aged 48, a lorry driver who lived in Abingdon Avenue, Northampton was arrested in connection with the murder of Daniella. When interviewed by police, McKenna denied ever knowing or meeting Daniella and vehemently denied being involved in her murder. During a forensic examination of a white Skoda belonging to McKenna, forensic experts found bloodstains on the back of the driver's seat and on the rear windscreen inside the vehicle, both of which matched blood samples taken from the victim. A fingerprint left by Daniella was found on a back seat of the car, and matching DNA samples were also found inside the vehicle. All the forensic evidence indicated that Daniella had been murdered in the back of McKenna's car before being driven the six miles to Blisworth and dumped onto the railway line during the early hours of the morning on 12 December 1995.

Philip Anthony McKenna was later charged with the wilful murder of Daniella White. He appeared before Northampton Magistrates Court on Friday 2 February 1996. He appeared in court dressed in a blue shirt and grey jacket. He said nothing, but stood motionless in the dock, and merely nodded as his name was read out. As the court discussed details of the case, McKenna's wife wept in the public gallery. The defendant was then remanded in custody to stand trial at Northampton Crown Court for the wilful murder of Daniella White. No application was made for bail.

In October 1997, the trial took place at Northampton Crown Court. McKenna denied murdering Daniella White. The presiding Judge was Mr Justice Francis Allen.

On Tuesday, 21 October, the jury retired to consider their verdict. After deliberating for five hours the jury returned a verdict of guilty by a majority verdict of ten to two. Following the verdict, the court heard that the defendant had previously appeared before Reading Crown Court in 1988 where he was convicted on several offences of gross indecency on a 12-year-old boy, indecent assault on a woman and also for threatening to kill a prostitute by holding a knife to her throat. For those offences, he had been sentenced to five years imprisonment.

There were cheers from members of Daniella's family who were sitting in the public gallery when the verdict was announced and the judge ordered her father, George White to leave the court after he started shouting abuse at McKenna. McKenna himself showed no remorse and little emotion as Judge Allen sentenced him to life imprisonment.

Stabbing in a Station Car Park

Khalid Mahmood was born in Pakistan in 1958. In 1978, he emigrated to England and settled in Bristol where he met Imtiaz Begum who became his wife. They went on to have four children; three girls and a boy, during which time Khalid worked as a part-time taxi driver.

In 1990, he started to accuse his wife Imtiaz of having an affair, although there was no evidence to support this. Their relationship became stormy, and Imtiaz started to complain of being physically abused by her husband. As tensions in the marriage increased, with continuous quarrelling and rowing between them taking place, Imtiaz left Khalid and fled to a women's hostel in Birmingham, taking their 18-month-old baby son with her.

Bristol County Court orders from 1994/95 showed that a tug-of-war custody fight took place over who should look after the four children. It was eventually agreed that their son Hasan would live with his mother in Birmingham, and Khalid would be allowed to travel to Birmingham on alternate Saturdays to visit his son during the afternoon. The three daughters remained at the family home in Bristol, living with their father.

On the morning of Saturday, 20 January 1996, Khalid Mahmood caught a train from Bristol to Birmingham on his fortnightly visit to see his son. He went to Birmingham New Street Station car park, where he had arranged to meet his estranged wife who was taking their son there in a hired car. Mahmood entered the car park shortly after midday and approached a Renault Clio. Imtiaz was sitting in the driver's seat, and Hasan was alongside her in the front passenger seat. As Khalid approached the car, Imtiaz opened the driver's door, got out of the car and handed him the car keys. Khalid then drove off with his son, having made the usual arrangements to bring him back to the car park a few hours later.

Later that afternoon, Khalid drove back into the station car park as planned and drove up to Imtiaz who was standing there waiting for him. Khalid got out of the car but when Imtiaz peered into the car, there was no sign of Hasan. She immediately started to panic and asked Khalid where Hasan was. Without warning, Khalid pulled out a knife and viciously attacked Imtiaz by repeatedly stabbing her in the chest in front of horrified onlookers. A probationary woman Police Constable, Jill Spencer, who was on duty nearby, witnessed the attack and with the assistance of 21-year- old Harry Robinson, a railway passenger who had just arrived, wrestled Khalid to the ground and disarmed him. Khalid was restrained and subsequently arrested. An ambulance was summoned for Imtiaz Begum but sadly she died from her stab wounds in the station car park before the ambulance arrived. Other police officers who had arrived on the scene made a further gruesome discovery. The dead body of 2-year-old Hasan Mahmood was found on the back seat of the car, covered by a blanket. He had been strangled to death by his father with a length of bandage which was still around his neck.

Following the arrest of Khalid Mahmood for the murder of his wife and son, concerns about the safety of his three daughters in Bristol were voiced and police officers from the Avon and Somerset Constabulary visited the terraced home of Mahmood in Montpelier, Bristol. After forcing their way into the house, another horrific discovery was made. The three girls, Saeqa, aged 14, Saema, aged 11 and Uzma, aged 9, were all found dead in their beds, with duvets covering their bodies. A postmortem later revealed that the three girls had each been given temazepam sleeping tablets which Mahmood had previously obtained for himself on prescription, then as they lay asleep in their beds, their throats had been cut with a large kitchen knife. All three girls had also been stabbed numerous times in their necks, causing them to bleed to death. It was estimated that they had been murdered the night before Khalid Mahmood made his trip to Birmingham. A bloodstained shirt belonging to Mahmood was found on the floor in an upstairs bathroom.

Mahmood was later charged with the wilful murder of his wife and their four children. He was remanded in custody to stand trial at Birmingham Crown Court.

In October 1996 the murder trial of Khalid Mahmood took place at Birmingham Crown Court. He pleaded not guilty on all five counts of wilful murder. Stephen Linehan QC, barrister for his defence argued that the mind of Mahmood had snapped because of the shame and anger he felt at being deserted by his wife, and although Mahmood did kill his five victims, he had no recollection of doing so, therefore the jury should find him guilty of manslaughter on the grounds of diminished responsibility, and not guilty of murder. The jury however disagreed, and on Wednesday, 9 October 1996, the fifth day of the trial, they found him guilty on all five counts of wilful murder, by unanimous decision.

During the trial, one juror fainted and was excused from the trial as graphic details unfolded on the savagery inflicted on the girls. Detective Chief Inspector Kevin Barry was named as the senior investigating officer.

After the jury reached their verdicts, the trial Judge, Mr Justice Butterfield told Mahmood. 'You have been convicted of five offences of murder. The law permits me to impose only one sentence, that of life imprisonment. That is the sentence I impose in respect of each count of murder.' Khalid Mahmood showed no emotion as the guilty verdicts were announced, or when the sentences were passed. He was then escorted from the dock.

Schoolgirl Battered to Death

During the afternoon on Sunday, 7 July 1996, Jade Matthews, a 9-year-old schoolgirl, left her home in Litherland, Merseyside to go out to play. She never returned. Police were informed of her disappearance and a full-scale search for the missing schoolgirl commenced the following morning. Several hours later, a police dog handler was searching a disused railway line when he found the body of Jade near some railway sidings in Bridle Road, Netherton, Bootle, just over a mile from the location where the battered body of toddler James Bulger had been found just three years earlier. Jade Matthews had also been beaten to death in a similar fashion to James Bulger and there were even suggestions of a copy-cat killing.

A murder investigation was set up which led to the arrest of a 13-year-old schoolboy Brian Smith who had been a friend of Jade Matthews. It was established that Smith had given a lift to Matthews on the back of his mountain bike on 7 July. He dropped her off not far from where her body was found, but he was adamant that she was safe and well when he dropped her off. Although detectives were not satisfied with his version of events, Smith stuck to his story for more than six months. Police continued to gather evidence until they were satisfied that they had sufficient evidence to charge Smith with the wilful murder of Jade Matthews.

Brian Smith, of Province Road, Bootle, Merseyside, appeared before Liverpool Crown Court on Friday 7 February 1997, where it was anticipated that he would plead not guilty to the charge of wilful murder. Smith however, dramatically changed his plea to guilty after making a last-minute tearful confession to a top psychiatrist, Doctor Susan Bailey.

The circumstances of the case were outlined, and the court was told that on the afternoon of Sunday, 7 July the previous year, Brian Smith was playing on his mountain bike with Jade, who was a schoolfriend of his younger brother. He took her on his bike to a disused railway line in Bridle Way, Netherton. When they arrived, the line was deserted and Jade became scared and asked to be taken home. Brian lost his temper and pushed her over causing her to bang her head which started to bleed. Jade told Brian that she was going to tell her parents what he had done to her, so he panicked and started beating her to prevent her from telling anyone that he had pushed her over.

The prosecution produced footage from a security video camera near the scene of the crime which had captured details of the murder as it unfolded. The footage was shown in court, and although the quality was extremely poor, it did capture 85 seconds of horrific images showing what had taken place. Smith was seen to pick up a wooden section of a broken window frame before repeatedly battering his helpless victim about the head and body until she lay motionless. She was clubbed to death with eight blows to the head and at least twenty blows to her body and arms as she tried to defend herself.

The Judge, Mr Justice Kay told Smith that he was a 'very dangerous boy', before sentencing him to be detained indefinitely. The Judge also stated that the utmost care must be taken before Smith was ever released, to make sure that he was no danger to anyone. Smith showed no emotion as he was led from the dock.

At 7.30am on Tuesday, 16 September 2003, Brian Smith was found unconscious and hanging by his neck in his cell at Aylesbury young offenders institute. He was rushed to a nearby hospital but was pronounced dead at 8.17am. The cause of death was later recorded as suicide. When he hanged himself, he was alone in a single cell and was on suicide watch which meant that he was being checked by a member of staff every half-hour.

The following day, Denise Matthews, Jade's mother, was informed by the probation service that Brian Smith had committed suicide. After hearing the news, Denise burst into tears and said:

> I am relieved that we will never have to worry about him coming out and doing the same thing again. He can't hurt anybody else. He can rot in hell now. I'm glad he's dead. I know it sounds terrible, but I feel justice has finally been done. Hopefully, Jade will be able to rest in peace. I can never forgive him for what he did, and I'll never understand why he did it. There was no excuse. No reason.

Man Pushed in Front of a Train

At about 7pm on Thursday, 18 February 1999, William Hichin visited Loughborough Railway Station in Leicestershire to meet his daughter Gwen, who was arriving by train after attending a job interview in London. As the train entered the station, William stepped back behind the yellow safety line on the platform as a precaution against the train doors being opened. When the train was about 30ft away from him, a man who was a complete stranger walked up behind him and pushed him violently on his shoulder blades, which caused William to totter forward, before falling over the edge of the platform and ending up lying face down on the track between the two running rails.

William raised his head and saw the train which was about 15ft away still travelling towards him. realising that he would be unable to get to his feet before being struck by the train, he managed to roll over, clear of the rails to avoid being run over. He was unsure whether his feet were clear of the rails, but fortunately they were as the train wheels passed close to his face. Due to his quick thinking, he had miraculously avoided almost certain death by a matter of seconds.

As William lay beneath the overhang of the train coaches, he turned his head again, and to his utter amazement he saw a young man (the man who had pushed him) lying beneath the train, unscathed as the train continued passing over him before coming to a sudden halt as the train driver applied the emergency brake. William looked at the young man in disbelief as he just laid there laughing at what had happened. William Hichin and the young man were quickly rescued from the track. Hichin suffered some minor cuts and bruises and was treated for shock but was not detained in hospital. The young man who had pushed him onto the railway line was unscathed and arrested by police on suspicion of attempted murder. He was taken into custody.

In July 1999, Benjamin Rathbone, aged 23, a paranoid schizophrenic who had previously received treatment for his illness by the Leicestershire Mental Health Service, appeared before Leicester Crown Court where he pleaded guilty to the attempted murder of William Hichin. He was detained by the judge for an indefinite period under the Mental Health Act.

Stabbed to Death During an Argument

On Tuesday, 28 December 1999, David Nigel Tillen, a 26-year-old soldier from Wendover Way, Witherwack, Sunderland, Tyne and Wear, was on home leave from the army whilst serving in Bosnia, when he visited Sunderland Railway Station with his younger sister and another girl.

Upon arrival, they entered a Burger King restaurant located on the station, for some light refreshments. Whilst inside the restaurant, an argument broke out between Tillen and 21-year-old Stephen Gibbon, a complete stranger, who was in the restaurant with his cousin, Graeme Scott. During the argument, Tillen suddenly produced a knife and stabbed Stephen Gibbon five times in the chest. Graeme Scott intervened to stop the attack, but his throat was slashed by Tillen, severing his windpipe and leaving him fighting for his life.

Police officers were quickly on the scene and Tillen was arrested. Graeme Scott was rushed to hospital and luckily, he survived the attack. Stephen Gibbon however was not so fortunate. After being stabbed in the chest by Tillen, he was conveyed to Sunderland Royal Hospital where he died shortly after his arrival.

Following his arrest, Tillen was charged with the murder of Stephen Gibbon and the attempted murder of Graeme Scott. In March 2000, Household Cavalry trooper David Tillen appeared before Sunderland Magistrates where he was remanded in custody and committed to stand trial at the Newcastle Crown Court.

In October, he appeared before Newcastle Crown Court where he pleaded not guilty to murder and attempted murder. Counsel for the defence argued that Tillen had been attacked by the two men and was acting in self-defence because he was scared and felt threatened. Other independent witnesses however testified that the defendant Tillen was the aggressor who made an unprovoked knife attack on Stephen Gibbon before slashing the throat of Graeme Scott who went to his cousin's aid.

On 26 October, it took the jury just over two hours to find Tillen guilty of murdering Stephen Gibbon and attempting to murder Graeme Scott. The trial judge Mr Justice Longmore sentenced Tillen to life imprisonment. The parents of Stephen Gibbon, the murder victim, broke down in tears in the public gallery as sentence was passed.

Chapter 8

Twenty-First Century

University Student Killed in a Drunken Brawl

On Friday, 2 March 2001, Patrick Brown, a 21-year-old second-year student at Durham University visited Newcastle with four of his undergraduate friends to celebrate a birthday of one of the young men.

After consuming copious amounts of alcohol, they went to Newcastle Railway Station and boarded the1.50am train back to Durham. Not long afterwards, another group of young men who had also been drinking boarded the train and sat in the same coach. During the journey to Durham, both groups were quite boisterous, and as the train approached Durham Station, one of the young men in Patrick Brown's group realised that his wallet was missing and suggested that one of the men from the other group had taken it. A drunken brawl then started between the two groups of young men.

At this point, the train arrived at Durham Station where all the young men alighted but the scruffles continued on the station platform. Patrick Brown was attacked and punched by 24-year-old Christopher Woolley of Bek Road, Durham, causing him to fall backwards, down a steep embankment, before landing on the A690 dual carriageway, some 20ft below. Sadly the fall was to prove fatal.

Andrew Zepher, a third-year undergraduate, and a close friend of Brown later told police, 'I just have flashbacks about what happened, but I have an image of my friend Patrick Brown, dying in a pool of his own blood.' Brown later died of injuries sustained in the fall after being punched by Christopher Woolley

After a police investigation was carried out, Christopher Woolley was charged with the wilful murder of Patrick Brown. He subsequently appeared at Newcastle Crown Court where he was cleared of murder but found guilty of manslaughter. After the verdict was announced, the court was told by the prosecutor, John Milford QC, that in February 1997, Christopher Woolley was convicted at Durham Crown Court of unlawful wounding with intent to do grievous bodily harm, after he was involved in a serious attack on two other university students in Durham Market Place. He was sentenced to serve two years in a young offenders' institution. Mr Milford went on to say that the seriousness of the first attack, together with the manslaughter conviction for this attack, made Woolley subject to a mandatory life sentence.

Christopher Woolley was subsequently sentenced to life imprisonment with a recommendation that he serve at least seven years. He was released from prison after serving just three years and nine months. The parents and family of Patrick Brown have constantly campaigned, without success, against the sentence handed out to Woolley, which they considered to be too lenient.

Schizophrenic Attempted to Push Passengers Under a Train

In May 2003, Christine Goldsmith, aged 33, an architect from London, and Tamlyn Monson, also aged 33, a production assistant from London, were both passengers standing on the Northern Line platform at Euston Underground Station, along with numerous other passengers, waiting to catch a train.

Suddenly, 40-year-old Christopher Studders walked up behind Goldsmith and pushed her forcefully in the back with both hands, propelling her forward. She fell off the platform edge onto the railway line. Although very shocked, and shaken by the fall, she was not electrocuted by the live rail, and did not suffer any serious injuries. She managed to struggle to her feet but became extremely frightened when she heard the sound of a train coming through the tunnel towards her. She started to scramble back onto the platform, assisted by other passengers, who grabbed both her arms and pulled her back onto the platform to safety. In the meantime, Christopher Studders had also attempted to push Tamlyn Monson onto the track, but fortunately, she had been grabbed by another passenger and pulled to safety as she tottered on the platform edge in front of the train which was entering the station platform. Both women had a very narrow escape.

Studders was overpowered by other passengers and detained until police officers arrived. He told passengers that he had intended to harm a child but then came up with the idea of pushing the two women under a train instead. Studders was subsequently arrested by police. After his arrest, it was established that Studders was a schizophrenic, who was receiving treatment at St Luke's Hospital, in North London, but he had been allowed out for the day.

In April 2004, Christopher Studders appeared before the Central Criminal Court in London charged with two counts of attempted murder. He pleaded not guilty on both counts but was found guilty by a unanimous decision of the jury. He was sentenced under the Mental Health Act to be confined in Chase Farm Hospital, North London for an indefinite period.

Islamist Terrorists Target London

At 8.50 am on Thursday, 7 July 2005, three bombs were detonated within seconds of each other by suicide bombers on the London Underground. The first bomb exploded on Circle line train number 204 as it travelled between Liverpool Street and Aldgate East. An adjacent track, the Hammersmith & City Line, was also damaged in the blast and had to be closed to traffic. Seven people, including the bomber, were killed in the blast and dozens more were injured.

The second bomb went off on another Circle line train, number 216, just after it departed from Edgware Road, travelling towards Paddington. The explosion also caused damage to another train which was passing in the opposite direction on an adjacent track. A tunnel wall was badly damaged by the blast and later collapsed. There were numerous casualties, and seven people (including the bomber) died.

A third bomb was detonated on Piccadilly line train number 311 which was travelling southbound between King's Cross and Russell Square Stations. Unlike the Circle line where the tunnels lie just below the surface of the city, the Piccadilly line tunnels are single track tunnels deep underground. Consequently, the blast of the explosion was more concentrated and had a much more devastating effect. This resulted in a vast number of casualties in which twenty-seven people, including the bomber, lost their lives.

Exactly one hour after the three bombs exploded on the underground network, a fourth explosion took place. This time, the target was a No. 30 double-decker bus which was travelling from Marble Arch to Hackney. The explosion occurred whilst the bus was in Upper Woburn Place near Tavistock Square in Central London. The roof of the bus was ripped off by the explosion and the rear portion of the bus was completely destroyed. A total of thirteen passengers and the bomber were killed by the blast. Dozens of others bus passengers and street pedestrians suffered injuries.

Police later announced that the explosions had been politically motivated terror attacks carried out by Islamist extremists. They were co-ordinated suicide attacks aimed at commuters travelling on London's public transport system during the morning rush hour. The terrorists who carried out the attacks were later named as: Hasib Hussain, aged 18 from Leeds, Mohammad Sidique Khan, aged 30 from Leeds, Germaine Lindsay, aged 19 from Aylesbury and Shehzad Tanweer, aged 22 from Leeds. Three of the bombers were British-born sons of Pakistani immigrants. The fourth, Lyndsay was born in Jamaica and later converted to Islam.

The four attacks resulted in the mass murder of fifty-two people of eighteen different nationalities. In addition, a further 784 people were injured in the attacks, many of them seriously. It was the first ever Islamist terrorist suicide attack to take place within the UK. All four perpetrators died whilst carrying out the attacks, and there were no criminal proceedings instituted against any other individuals in connection with these terrible atrocities.

Woman Tortured and Beaten to Death

Shortly after daybreak on Monday, 9 August 2010, John Irving was out jogging along a disused railway line in Rugby, Warwickshire, when he came across the naked body of a young woman, lying face down on a grass verge at a location called the Old Station. Mr Irving immediately contacted the police who visited the scene, before setting up a murder investigation. The body was later identified as that of a 27-year-old local woman, Gemma Hayter.

Following a lengthy police investigation conducted by Detective Chief Inspector James Essex and officers of the Warwickshire Constabulary,

Daniel Newstead, aged 20, Joe Samuel Boyer, aged 18, Chantelle Franklyn Booth, aged 20, and Jessica Lynas, aged 19, all residents of Little Pennington Street, Rugby, together with Duncan Edwards, aged 19, of Ashwood Court, Rugby, were all arrested on suspicion of the wilful murder of Gemma Hayter. The five accused were subsequently committed to stand trial at Warwick Crown Court in July 2011 on various criminal charges to which they pleaded not guilty.

During the trial, the court was told that the victim Gemma Hayter was a vulnerable young woman with learning disabilities, who was often teased and tormented by the five defendants who she considered to be her friends. On 8 August 2010, Gemma visited a flat in Rugby where she met her so called friends. During the evening the five accused started to torment and bully Gemma. As the evening progressed, the abuse became physical, and Gemma was beaten and tortured by the five accused, in which she suffered a broken nose. She was forced to drink wine, before two of the accused, Duncan Edwards and Joe Boyer both urinated into a can of lager then forced Miss Hayter to drink it. Miss Hayter tried to use her mobile phone to summon help, but that was taken from her and flushed down a toilet to prevent her from using it. Gemma was then locked in another room to prevent her leaving the flat.

In the early hours of Monday, 9 August, Gemma was taken out of the flat and led along the deserted streets like a faithful dog. She was taken to the disused railway site of the old station. There, the physical abuse began again. Gemma was kicked, slashed with a knife and a plastic bag was forced over her head. She screamed, struggled and tried to fight off her attackers until she eventually choked to death on her own blood. She was then stripped naked before being left on the grass verge where her body was later found.

The trial judge, Lady Justice Rafferty remarked during the trial, 'The vile torture and murder of Miss Hayter was a chronicle of heartlessness. I struggle to see how much lower you could have sunk. It is difficult to find the words to express how vile your behaviour was'. She went on to say that 'Over the years you treated Gemma Hayter like a toy to be picked up and put down, dependent, I suspect, on whether there was a gap in your miserable life which she could fill.' Judge Rafferty singled out the defendant Booth as 'a nasty piece of work' whom Miss Hayter had described as her best friend. None of the five accused tried to stop the murder from happening, and not one of them reported it.

Following the trial, the jury retired to consider their verdicts before returning to announce their verdicts as follows. Daniel Newstead, Chantelle Franklyn Booth, and Joe Samuel Boyer were each found guilty of the wilful murder of Gemma Hayter. They were all sentenced to life imprisonment. The judge, Lady Justice Rafferty, ordered Booth to serve at least twenty-one years, while Newstead was ordered to serve at least twenty years. Joe Samuel Boyer was ordered to serve at least sixteen years in prison.

The two other defendants, Jessica Lynas and Duncan Edwards were found not guilty of wilful murder, but guilty of manslaughter. Lynas was sentenced to serve thirteen years imprisonment and Edwards was sentenced to serve fifteen years imprisonment.

Not one of the defendants showed any remorse for being involved in this horrific crime.

Passenger Pushed Under a Moving Train

At 11.40 am on Wednesday 2 December 2015, Kamlesh Ramji, aged 40, was standing on the southbound platform at Kentish Town Underground Station in London, waiting to catch a train. As a train approached the platform, Mr Ramji was pushed violently from behind, pushing him forward to the platform edge where he fell onto the track in front of horrified passengers.

Mr Ramji was then struck by the approaching train, which passed over his body which was lying on the track in between the two running rails. Mr Ramji was rendered unconscious and rushed by ambulance to hospital suffering from serious injuries which included a fractured skull, brain injuries, fractured ribs, a punctured lung, shattered pelvis and internal injuries. He remained in a coma, in a critical condition for almost a month, before regaining consciousness on Christmas Eve. It was a miracle that he survived his ordeal although doctors informed him that he would never make a full recovery from his injuries which would affect both his career and his independence for the rest of his life.

There were a number of witnesses to the incident who stated that a man just walked up behind Mr Rami and for no apparent reason, shoved him off the platform in front of the approaching train, by pushing his shoulder blades. The man then sprinted onto the northbound platform and fled the scene. The whole incident was recorded on the station CCTV.

A description of the offender was circulated, and a police manhunt was soon underway. Later that day, 29-year-old Devindra Ferguson from Colindale, North West London, went into Lewisham Police Station in South-East London and told police that he was the man that they were seeking for pushing someone under a train at Kentish Town that morning. Ferguson was formally arrested.

Enquiries revealed that Ferguson had a history of mental illness after being diagnosed as a paranoid schizophrenic. He told police that the victim Ramji was a complete stranger to him. He refused to reveal a motive for the attack, saying, 'All you need to know is that it was my intention to do it.'

Devindra Ferguson was subsequently charged with the attempted murder of Kamlesh which concluded with a trial at Blackfriars Crown Court in London where he admitted attempted murder and was detained indefinitely in a secure mental institution. The trial judge, Justice Peter Clarke said: 'Ferguson was a danger to everyone, including himself.' In the unlikely event of an improvement in his health, Ferguson of Parklea Close, Colindale could be brought back before the courts to be sentenced to a lengthy term of imprisonment.

Attacked Passengers with a Bread Knife

Muhaydin Mire, aged 29, moved to the UK from Somalia as a child and was brought up living in Leytonstone in East-London.

Shortly after 7pm on Saturday, 5 December 2015, Mire alighted from an underground train at Leytonstone tube station, and as he walked towards the exit barriers in the ticket hall, he produced a bread knife from beneath his jacket and ran amok amongst other passengers who were also leaving the station. Mire started attacking passengers at random whilst brandishing the bread knife. One of the victims who Mire targeted was Lyle Zimmerman, aged 56, who was carrying a mandolin and had a guitar strapped to his back. Mire attacked Zimmerman from behind, dragging him onto the floor before slashing him three times across his neck in a 'sawing motion' with the knife, cutting his throat and exposing his trachea, whilst shouting, 'This is for my Syrian brothers.'

Louise McGuinness, another passenger, shouted at Mire to stop, but he started to kick Zimmerman before turning to Miss McGuinness and saying, 'This is for telling me to stop.' Miss McGuinnes again shouted, 'Stop it, stop it,' but Mire told her, 'You're next.'

Daniel Bielinski, a Polish passenger and another man also intervened, and Mire attempted to stab them both with the knife. Fortunately, police officers who had been summoned were quickly on the scene and used a taser device to incapacitate Mire before arresting him. An off-duty junior doctor, Matthew Smith, who was passing through the station during the incident, was able to treat Lyle Zimmerman who was lying in a pool of blood. It later transpired that the prompt action by Dr Smith prior to the arrival of an ambulance saved the life of Mr Zimmerman who had been bleeding to death from the wounds on his neck.

Muhaydin Mire was subsequently arrested and later charged with attempted murder of Zimmerman and attempting to injure four others.

Scotland Yard initially classified the attack as an act of terrorism with connections to Islamic State but after consultation with medical experts, decided that Mire's violence resulted from his acute mental health problems rather than political motivation. It transpired that Mire had a history of mental illness and was experiencing paranoid delusions a month before the attack, He had failed to attend an appointment with a community mental health team just four days before the attack.

Mire later appeared before the Old Bailey, where he pleaded not guilty to the attempted murder of Lyle Zimmerman, but pleaded guilty to unlawfully wounding Zimmerman and attempting to injure four others. The jury however found Mire guilty of attempted murder, and he was sentenced to life imprisonment.

Passenger Stabbed on a Train

On Monday, 12 December 2016, Adrian Brown, aged 38, left a hostel in Brockley Rise, Forest Hill, South East London where he was living, and walked a short distance to Honor Oak Park Station where he boarded a train. He was in possession of a knife, and it was his intention to find and kill Muslim men.

Shortly after the train departed, Brown got up from his seat brandishing the knife and walked up and down the train, threatening death to Muslims whilst looking for Muslim men to stab and kill.

As he walked through the train, he saw Muhammed Ali, who was sitting next to his wife. Without warning, Brown approached Ali and repeatedly stabbed him in his head and body. Mr Ali's wife screamed as other passengers intervened to restrain Brown. An off-duty doctor and nurse who happened to be travelling on the train also rushed over and gave medical attention to Mr Ali who was bleeding profusely from his stab wounds, one of which had punctured his lung, causing breathing difficulties.

After passengers had pulled Brown away from Mr Ali, he broke free and held the knife to the throat of a woman passenger and shouted, 'Where are all the Muslims? I am going to kill all the Muslims.' The woman managed to wriggle free from Brown and fortunately she did not suffer any physical injuries.

The train then arrived at Forest Hill Station where Brown alighted and left the station followed by some of the passengers who alerted the police. A description of Brown was circulated, and he was arrested not far from the station shortly afterwards. He was still holding the knife when David Pearson, an off-duty police officer told him to put down the knife. Brown told the officer, 'No but you are safe, you're a Christian.'

Following his arrest, Brown was deemed to be suffering from schizophrenia and was conveyed to Broadmoor Hospital where he was detained.

The trial of Adrian Brown took place at Southwark Crown Court in London, where he faced charges of attempting to murder Muhammed Ali, being in possession of an offensive weapon and other offences. Brown, wearing a brown tracksuit, appeared via video link from Broadmoor Hospital where he was still being detained. He pleaded not-guilty to all the charges and was found not-guilty on all charges by reason of insanity.

Detaining Brown indefinitely under section 37 of the Mental Health Act, Judge Deborah Taylor QC said:

> You have a long history of psychotic illness and on that day, you were suffering, and you continue to suffer from paranoid schizophrenia. … You attempted to kill Mr Ali by stabbing him repeatedly. There is no doubt that if it had not been for the intervention of two medical practitioners, he may well have died. Such were the severity of his injuries and the loss of blood.

Brown can only ever be released from hospital on the order of a judge or the Secretary of State.

Man Died During an Altercation

At approximately 12.30am on Tuesday, 29 August 2017, Terry Bailey, aged 39, was sitting on the pavement outside Leeds City Railway Station. Although he had an address in South-Leeds, Bailey frequently slept rough in the city centre, often in the vicinity of the railway station. Whilst sitting on the pavement, two men, Daniel Goodall, aged 42, and Jamie Loftus, aged 28, walked past him on their way to the station taxi-rank. As they walked past Bailey, one of the men made a remark to him and a verbal altercation ensued. The two men walked away but Bailey followed them to the taxi rank where the altercation continued as the men got into a taxi. Bailey shook his fist and started banging the taxi door.

One of the men, Jamie Loftus then alighted from the taxi but was attacked by Bailey and a fight broke out during which Bailey was punched by Loftus. The other man, Daniel Goodall then alighted from the cab and appeared to join in the attack. Bailey eventually fell to the ground, banging his head on the side of the pavement as he fell. Goodall and Loftus then walked away, leaving Bailey lying in the gutter.

The taxi driver summoned police, and an ambulance was called to convey Bailey to hospital, where he was pronounced dead shortly after his arrival. Mr Bailey's father and brother were subsequently informed of his death.

Daniel Goodall and Jamie Loftus were later arrested by police on suspicion of murder and detectives examined CCTV footage of the incident as part of their ongoing investigation. The two men were later charged with the manslaughter of Terry Bailey, and they were committed to stand trial at Leeds Crown Court.

In February 2018, the trial of Goodall and Loftus took place at Leeds Crown Court. The jury heard that the accused men both knew Terry Bailey and the altercation which took place related to a dispute over drugs.

At the time of the incident, Goodall and Loftus were catching a taxi to go to Beeston to buy and take drugs. The jury was shown CCTV footage of the whole incident as it unfolded and the court heard that after Bailey started banging on the taxi door, Loftus got out of the taxi to continue the altercation with Bailey but he came under attack from Bailey, so he punched Bailey in the head. The court was told that Goodall then got out of the taxi, not to join in the attack, but to separate the two men and act as peacemaker in the argument. It was then that Bailey was pushed away from Goodall, but fell to the floor, striking his head on the pavement.

Goodall told the court that Bailey had been his friend since school, and he had no intention of hurting him. Loftus also gave evidence on oath saying that he only threw a punch at Bailey as he feared for his own safety after coming under attack from Bailey.

On 9 February 2018, following a seven-day trial, the jury reached a unanimous verdict that Bailey instigated the altercation and showed aggression towards Loftus. They found Jamie Loftus and Daniel Goodall not-guilty of manslaughter and the two accused walked free from court.

Passenger Attacked Going Home

On 5 November 2017, Samir Draganovic, aged 23, alighted from a train at Knockholt Station in Kent on his way home from work. Shortly after alighting from the train, a man who was a complete stranger, came running along the platform towards him brandishing a knife. Fearing for his own safety, Draganovic turned away from the man and ran in the opposite direction.

The man with the knife continued chasing Draganovic, who ran off the end of the platform onto the railway track, followed by his assailant. There, the attacker caught up with Draganovic and subjected him to a frenzied knife attack, as a result of which Draganovic died from multiple stab wounds and was left lying on the side of the railway line. Footage of the incident was captured on CCTV installed at the railway station.

Not long afterwards, the victim's body was spotted by a passing train driver. Police were informed and a murder investigation was set up by Detective Chief Inspector Paul Langley of the British Transport Police.

An extensive police investigation eventually led to the arrest of Jamie Simmons, aged 37, of Blackfriars Road, Southwark. When interviewed by police, Simmons denied killing Draganovic and denied being anywhere near Knockholt Station on the day in question. When shown CCTV footage of the incident, he denied being the person in the footage. Data from his personal mobile phone proved that he was in the vicinity of the station at the time of the murder but again he denied being there.

Simmons was later charged with the wilful murder of Samir Draganovic, and his trial took place the Inner London Crown Court in May 2018, where he attempted to plead guilty to manslaughter due to diminished responsibility, saying he could not remember the incident.

This was not accepted by the prosecution and his trial for murder continued. On the second day of his trial, he finally admitted that he was at Knockholt Station on the day in question, and he was responsible for the death of Draganovic, but maintained that he was not guilty of murder as he could not recall anything about the incident.

The trial lasted five days and the evidence against Simmons was compelling. At the conclusion of the trial, the jury retired for 90 minutes before returning a verdict of guilty.

Simmons was sentenced to life imprisonment with a recommendation that he should serve a minimum of twenty-six years in prison. It was never established why the brutal attack and murder of the young man took place. There seemed to be no apparent motive for the attack which seemed to have been entirely random. Samir Draganovic was just a young man travelling home from work.

Following his conviction, Simmons was incarcerated at Swaleside Prison on the Isle of Sheppey in Kent where, on 26 February 2022 he was found hanging in his cell after attempting to commit suicide. Simmons was conveyed to hospital, but he died a week later.

Attempt to Kill Two Passengers

On 5 October 2018, Paul Crossley, aged 46, was found guilty of two counts of attempted murder when he appeared before the Central Criminal Court in London. He had pleaded not guilty to both charges.

The first victim was 91-year-old Sir Robert Malpas, a former Eurotunnel boss who, in April 2018, was walking along the platform at Marble Arch Underground Station, smartly dressed in a suit and wearing a Burberry raincoat. He was carrying an umbrella. Suddenly, without warning, Crossley, who was wearing a hooded garment with the hood pulled over his cap, approached Sir Robert from behind, and pushed him from the station platform onto the track just sixty seconds before a train was due to arrive.

Ryiad El-Hussani, a passenger who was standing further along the platform, heard 'screams and shouting', before sprinting 20 metres and leaping onto the tracks, to drag Sir Robert off the railway lines. He noticed that Sir Robert's clothes and umbrella were covered in blood, before managing to lift him onto the platform to safety. Mr El-Hussani then managed to clamber back onto the platform himself, just as a train entered the station. He suffered a badly burned arm after coming into contact with the live rail whilst he rescued Sir Robert. The whole incident was captured on footage by a CCTV camera situated on the station platform. During his fall from the platform, Sir Robert himself suffered severe injuries which included a fractured pelvis and a gash to the head which required twelve stitches. The judge later praised Mr El-Hussani for showing 'extraordinary bravery with a complete disregard for his own safety in saving the life of Sir Robert'.

The court also heard that a second passenger, Tobias French, just managed to keep his balance when he had been pushed in the back by Crossley just as a train was pulling into Tottenham Court Road Station, earlier the same day. Mr French told the court that he just managed to stop himself falling from the platform and remembered thinking that he had a lucky escape and was very lucky to be alive.

Following police enquiries, Paul Crossley was arrested in connection with the two incidents. He told police that on the day before the incidents, he had taken crack cocaine and had hardly slept that night. This he said, caused him to have panic attacks, during which he pushed both men from behind. He stated that all he meant to do was to push them onto the floor as a bit of fun. Crossley told the jury that he had selected both his victims at random, but he did not intend to kill either of them.

Following his conviction by the jury, Crossley was sentenced to life imprisonment on both counts of attempted murder. After the jury was dismissed, Crossley sobbed and removed his glasses to wipe away the tears before being led from the dock.

Knife Attack by Terrorist Sympathiser

At about 9pm on New Year's Eve 2018, Mahdi Mohamud, aged 26 of Cheetham Hill, Manchester visited Manchester Victoria Railway Station armed with two kitchen knives concealed in a waistband beneath his coat. His intention was to attack and kill random passengers who were using the railway station.

As he planned his attack, he saw a man and a woman, James Knox and Anna Charlton, both in their fifties, walking towards the tram platform. Mohamud walked up behind the couple shouting 'Allahu Akbar' and 'Long live the caliphate'. He then repeatedly stabbed James Knox in the back, shoulders and head. Knox fell to the ground with blood pouring from his wounds. Anna Charlton screamed and turned around, but Mohamud slashed her across the forehead with the kitchen knife, before stabbing her violently in the chest. During the vicious attacks, James Knox suffered thirteen separate injuries including a fractured skull, and Anna Charlton's right lung was punctured and the slash to her forehead cut into the bone.

At the time of the attack, a British Transport Police Sergeant, Lee Valentine, aged 31, was standing in uniform, some distance away on the tram platform, in conversation with some tram staff members when he heard a commotion before turning round and witnessing the attacks. Sergeant Valentine and the tram staff ran to where the attacks were taking place. Sergeant Valentine shot Mohamud with his taser, but the barbs got stuck in the knifeman's coat and failed to subdue him. Mohamud then attacked Valentine and stabbed him in the shoulder before being wrestled to the ground whilst still wielding the knife.

Mohamud was eventually restrained, and the second knife was removed from his waistband before he was arrested and taken into custody. James Knox and Anna Charlton and Sergeant Valentine were all conveyed to hospital for treatment to their wounds.

Mohamud was later sectioned under the Mental Health Act and detained in a secure mental health facility. A search of his home was carried out by Greater Manchester Police and officers recovered a large amount of 'counter-terrorism mindset material', which included documents and images on how to carry out knife attacks.

It was later established that Mahdi Mohamud was a Dutch national, born in Arnhem to Somali parents. The family moved to Britain in 2004 when he was aged nine. He attended school in Manchester before attending Leeds University where he obtained a degree in mechanical engineering. He later became radicalised online before suffering mental illness. He was first admitted to a UK hospital for mental health issues in December 2015.

Later he moved to East Africa and was admitted to institutions in Somalia on three occasions in 2017, during which time he swung an axe at a nurse and stabbed a second nurse with a knife in a separate attack. He also stabbed his uncle.

Returning to the stabbing incident in Manchester, Mahdi Mohamud was subsequently charged with three counts of attempted murder, namely James Knox, Anna Charlton and Sergeant Lee Valentine. He was further charged with a terrorist offence involving the possession of Islamic State documents which were recovered from his home.

In November 2019, Mohamud appeared before Mr Justice Stuart-Smith at Manchester Crown Court where he pleaded guilty to all the charges. He was sentenced as follows:

Terrorism Act Offence. Four Years in custody.

Attempted Murder of James Knox. Life imprisonment with a minimum term of eleven years.

Attempted Murder of Anna Charlton. Life imprisonment with a minimum term of eleven years, concurrent.

Attempted Murder of Lee Valentine. Life imprisonment with a minimum term of eleven years, concurrent.

In addition, the judge Mr Justice Stuart-Smith made an order pursuant to section 45A of the Mental Health Act.

He said that instead of being removed and detained in prison, he will be detained at Ashworth High Security Hospital in Liverpool.

Passenger Stabbed in Railway Carriage

On Friday, 4 January 2019, Lee Pomeroy, aged 51, went to London Road Railway Station at Guildford in Surrey in company with his 14-year-old son. There, they boarded the 1pm train to London Waterloo. Mr Pomeroy and his son walked down the centre aisle of the train to find a suitable place to sit down. As they did so, Darren Pencille, aged 36, who had also boarded the train at Guildford, was walking along the aisle in the opposite direction, and as they came face to face, Pencille remarked that Pomeroy and his son were blocking his way through the aisle. An argument ensued and Pencille started swearing and using bad language. Pomeroy asked for an apology, but Pencille pulled out a knife and stabbed Pomeroy in the neck, severing the jugular vein. Pencille continued to stab Pomeroy in a frenzied and fatal attack which lasted for some thirty seconds. Pomeroy was stabbed eighteen times during the frantic attack and despite first aid being rendered by other passengers on the train, he died almost immediately.

Following the attack, the train pulled into Clandon Station where Pencille hastily alighted from the train and fled. The whole incident was captured on a CCTV camera installed in the train carriage. The train departed Clandon whilst the victim's son, who was in a state of severe shock, knelt over the body of his father. Police were alerted to the stabbing when the train arrived at the next station stop which was Horsley a few minutes later.

After getting off the train at Clandon, Pencille telephoned his girlfriend Chelsea Mitchell who lived in Farnham. Pencille informed her that he had been in an altercation on the train and asked for her assistance. Mitchell went by car to Clandon where she picked up Pencille and drove him back to her flat in Farnham where they had been living together. Upon arrival at the flat, Pencille had a shower and shaved off his beard, before disposing of his bloodstained clothing. Mitchell later conveyed Pencille to Bognor Regis in West Sussex by car, where he had a flat of his own. The couple stayed in the flat overnight, but they were both arrested by police who visited the flat in the early hours of the following morning. Pencille had earlier been identified as the attacker from the CCTV footage of the incident.

Pencille was later charged with the wilful murder of Lee Pomeroy, and Mitchell was charged with assisting an offender.

In July 2019, Pencille and Mitchell stood trial at the Central Criminal Court in London. Both pleaded not guilty to the charges brought against them. Pencille claimed that when he stabbed Pomeroy, he was acting in self-defence and did not intend to kill him. The jury was shown the CCTV footage of the incident which clearly showed that his version of events was not true.

On 12 July 2019, Darren Pencille and Chelsea Mitchell were both found guilty by the jury. Pencille was sentenced to life imprisonment with a recommendation that he should serve a minimum term of twenty-eight years. Mitchell was sentenced to serve twenty-eight months imprisonment for her part, which the judge described as a misguided loyalty to Pencille.

After the verdicts were announced, the court heard that Pencille, who had declined to give evidence during his trial, had fourteen previous convictions for nineteen different offences over a nineteen-year period, including possession of offensive weapons, violence and dishonesty. In 2010, he had stabbed a flatmate in the neck after a minor disagreement.

Chelsea Mitchell had seven previous convictions for ten different offences, including assault and battery, threatening behaviour and being drunk and disorderly.

Stabbed to Death by Rival Gang Member

At about 4.30pm on Monday, 27 January 2020, Louis Johnson aged 16 from South Norwood, London went to East Croydon Railway Station to catch a train. After entering the station via the Ruskin Square ticket barrier, he encountered Kion McKenna, also aged 16, from New Addington, Croydon. Both youths had known each other for almost three years as a result of being gang-members in rival gangs. Johnson belonged to a street-gang in Clapham, whilst McKenna was the member of another gang in Tooting. There had been friction between the two gangs for some time, and the two youths had crossed paths on at least three previous occasions. Both youths had previously been in trouble with the police for carrying knives.

Moments after Johnson entered the busy station, he was attacked by McKenna who pulled out a zombie knife and stabbed him repeatedly. Johnson eventually slumped to the ground and died in the arms of a commuter who had rushed to his aid whilst he was being attacked. McKenna ran out of the station and fled the scene in a taxi. The whole incident was recorded by a CCTV camera installed at the station.

After fleeing the scene, McKenna attempted to disguise himself by shaving off his long hair, but when it was announced that he was wanted by police in connection with the stabbing, he handed himself into a British Transport Police Station. When interviewed, McKenna told police, 'I didn't mean to kill Louis. I only stabbed him because I thought he was going to stab me'.

Kion McKenna was later charged with the wilful murder of Louis Johnson and being in possession of an offensive weapon. He was subsequently remanded in custody whilst waiting to stand trial at the Central Criminal Court in London.

Whilst incarcerated, he boasted that he first started carrying a knife at the age of 13, and he also wrote a rap song about his knife attack on Johnson.

In September 2020, Kion McKenna appeared before Mr Justice Mark Dennis QC at the Central Criminal Court where he pleaded guilty to being in possession of an offensive weapon, but not guilty to the wilful murder of Louise Johnson. At the conclusion of the trial, the jury found him guilty as charged.

Kion McKenna was sentenced to life imprisonment and the Judge recommended that he serve a minimum of sixteen years. Judge Dennis said of McKenna, 'Composing and sharing rap lyrics appeared to be him bragging about the killing, and by supporting and encouraging gang violence, demonstrated he had little concern about publicising his actions.' Judge Dennis went on to say, 'This was a shocking and dreadful display of violence for which there was no justification or excuse.' He told McKenna, 'Though you were of a young age, you were old enough to know what you were doing and able to make your own choices.'

Schoolboy Stabbed at Glasgow Station

On Saturday, 16 October 2021, Daniel Haig, aged 16, followed a group of schoolboys who were a couple of years younger than himself, to Glasgow High Street Railway Station. He was carrying a rucksack which contained a knife. Haig later told police that he was carrying the knife for protection, claiming that he had been attacked the previous day.

After arriving at the station, Haig approached the schoolboys as they stood chatting amongst themselves. Haig then started to intimidate and bully the boys, causing a scuffle to break out. Suddenly, Haig pulled the knife out of his rucksack and started threatening the boys. The boys immediately turned and ran away. Haig chased after the boys, brandishing his knife. As the boys dispersed, one of them, Justin McLaughlin, who had attained the age of 14 just two days earlier, tripped and fell to the ground. He managed to get to his feet but before he could escape, Haig caught up with him, attacked him and stabbed him in the chest. McLaughlin slumped to the ground, crying out for his mother. The other schoolboys had already left the scene. The whole incident was captured by CCTV cameras installed at the railway station.

Following the stabbing, Haig withdrew the knife from his victim and fled the railway station before disposing of the knife in a litter bin. It was later recovered by police. The emergency services were contacted by railway staff, and they arrived on the scene within minutes. McLaughlin was rushed to hospital by ambulance but died a short time later as a direct result of a stab wound to the heart.

A murder investigation was subsequently carried out and Daniel Haig was arrested. He admitted stabbing McLaughlin but stated that he had no intention of killing anyone. He said, 'I tried to aim for the lower part of his body, thinking it would just cause a minor injury.'

In August 2023, Daniel Haig, then aged 18, appeared before Judge Lord Clark at the High Court in Edinburgh, charged with the wilful murder of Justin McLaughlin. He pleaded not guilty. Following the trial, Haig was found guilty of murder and sentenced to life imprisonment. The Judge recommended that Haig serve a minimum of sixteen years imprisonment.

In July 2024, an appeal was heard at the Court of Criminal Appeal in Edinburgh, as to the severity of the sixteen years minimum sentence imposed by the trial judge Lord Clark, at the High Court where Haig had been convicted the previous year. The three appeal court judges upheld the appeal and reduced the sixteen year minimum sentence to thirteen years.

Pushed a Postman onto the Railway Track

On Saturday, 3 February 2024, Tadeusz Potoczek, a 61-year-old postman went to Oxford Circus Underground Station in London to catch a train home after finishing work. As he walked along the southbound Victoria Line platform, he walked past Brwa Shorsh, aged 24, a homeless Kurdish migrant from Northern Iraq, who was lying on a bench. Suddenly, without any warning or provocation, Shorsh sat up, leapt to his feet, then ran up behind Potoczek and pushed him violently in his back, causing him to fall onto the track just as a train was entering the station platform from the tunnel. As the train approached, Potoczek managed to scramble to his feet and was pulled back onto the platform by a quick-thinking passerby. Miraculously, Potoczek avoided being struck by the train and was not seriously hurt. Footage of the incident was recorded on CCTV installed on the station platform.

Although police officers were on the scene within minutes, they were informed by witnesses that the perpetrator had already fled the platform. He was however arrested later by British Transport Police officers at Warren Street Underground Station. When interviewed, he admitted pushing Potoczek from the platform but told officers that he had not seen the train coming and it was not his intention to kill him. He went on to say that he was very angry as he lay on the seat because three women had allegedly sniggered and passed comments about him for being homeless, and when Mr Potoczek walked past, he felt that he too had given him a dirty look, so he wanted to give him a fright, but not kill him. Brwa Shorsh was subsequently charged with the attempted murder of Tadeusz Potoczek and remanded in custody.

In July, Shorsh appeared before the Inner London Crown Court where he denied attempted murder. The court was told that Shorsh had been homeless and sleeping rough in London since 2020, often using underground stations because they provided shelter. The jury also heard that on 3 February he had intentionally pushed the victim from the station platform into the path of an oncoming train. Miraculously, with the assistance of another passenger he had managed to scramble to safety just before the train reached him. The driver of the train told the court that although he applied the emergency brakes, his train only just missed the man with one or two seconds to spare. CCTV footage of the whole incident was shown in court.

Shorsh still maintained that he had not seen the train coming and just wanted to give his victim a fright because he was angry. He said, 'In that split second I wanted revenge.' Throughout the trial however, Shorsh seemed to be amused by the proceedings and just stood in the dock smirking and smiling. He did not show any remorse for his actions.

At the conclusion of the trial, it took the jury just thirty minutes to find Shorsh guilty of attempted murder. Sentence was postponed to a later date pending various reports.

The quick-thinking individual who had assisted in rescuing Potoczek from the path of the moving train was commended by the judge, Benedict Kelleher, who awarded him £1,000 for his bravery and quick reaction.

On Thursday, 10 October 2024, Brwa Shorsh appeared before the Inner London Crown Court, where he was sentenced to life imprisonment, with a recommendation that he should serve a minimum of eight years.

Brwa Shorsh first entered Britain in 2018 when he was smuggled into the country in the back of a lorry after being denied asylum in Germany. He had racked up thirteen criminal convictions between 2018 and 2024. In 2020, a bid to have him deported was launched, at which time he declared himself homeless and went to live rough on the streets of London, presumably to avoid deportation.

Hotel Worker Stabbed with a Screwdriver

Deng Chol Majek, aged 18, from the Republic of Sudan in North East Africa, came to Britain in July 2024 as an illegal immigrant after crossing the English Channel in a small boat from France. Upon arrival in the UK, he immediately applied for political asylum despite having no passport, documentation or any form of identification. He spoke very little English, and an interpreter was engaged to enable him to communicate with the authorities.

Majek was subsequently transported to Bescot near Walsall in the West Midlands where he was given accommodation at the Park Hotel which was in close proximity to Walsall football stadium. The hotel was to be his home until such time that his asylum application could be processed.

During the early evening of Sunday, 20 December 2024, Majek was inside the Park Hotel when, he became involved in an altercation with 27-year-old Rhiannon Skye Whyte who was a member of the staff working at the hotel. The altercation was of a relatively minor nature, which started after Majek was found in the hotel kitchen, helping himself to packets of biscuits.

At 11pm that evening, Miss Whyte finished her shift and walked a short distance to Bescot Stadium Railway Station to catch the 11.21pm train home to Walsall where she lived with her mother. As she waited for her train to arrive, Miss Whyte telephoned a friend on her mobile phone, and whilst engaged in a conversation, she was attacked without warning by Majek, who it appears had followed her from the hotel to the railway station.

Majek, who was armed with a screwdriver stabbed Miss Whyte in the neck, before carrying out a vicious attack, mainly concentrated around her face and head. Miss Whyte fell to the ground as Majek fled the scene. She was found lying unconscious a few minutes later by another train passenger who summoned the emergency services.

Police officers and an ambulance quickly arrived on the scene. Miss Whyte was conveyed to Queen Elizabeth Hospital in Birmingham where she remained in a critical condition, having suffered severe damage to the brain. She remained unconscious for three days but sadly she died on Wednesday, 23 December. Her devastated family were at her bedside.

Following the incident, Majek was swiftly arrested by police and interviews were conducted via an interpreter. Majek denied stabbing or assaulting Miss Whyte and denied being at Bescot Railway Station. He was initially charged with attempting to murder Miss Whyte, but following her death, he was charged with her wilful murder. He was also charged with possessing an offensive weapon, namely the screwdriver which was used in the stabbing.

Majek appeared before Wolverhampton Magistrates Court before being remanded in custody at Manchester Prison. On 19 November 2024, Majek appeared by video link at Wolverhampton Magistrates Court where he was committed to stand trial for the murder of Rhiannon Whyte at Wolverhampton Crown Court on 19 November 2025. Majek is currently in custody awaiting trial.

Stabbed Partner During a Tiff

During the summer of 2024, Jason Flore, aged 26, originally from Mauritius, was sleeping rough in a tent in a disused station car park at Crawley Railway Station in West Sussex, with his partner, 19-year-old Stephanie Marie and their pet dog. The couple had known each other for over four years and were both of no fixed abode.

On Sunday, 18 August 2024, just after 7am, the couple were in the car park when a quarrel broke out between them. Flore and Marie were both quite drunk after drinking heavily at a barbecue the previous evening. The quarrel became belligerent, and a female witness who was standing on an overbridge saw Flore waving his hands and shouting in an aggressive manner at Marie, who appeared to be visibly upset and distressed. Flore then produced a knife and stabbed her in the chest several times, puncturing her heart and the aorta. The witness who saw the incident unfolding filmed video footage of the incident on her iPhone. After the attack, Flore who was wearing a red jacket and jogging trousers, walked out of the car park, accompanied by his dog, leaving his girlfriend lying on the ground where she had fallen after being stabbed. Flore then walked to a nearby bus stop and attempted to catch a bus, but was he was refused admission, so he walked off in the direction of the town centre.

In the meantime, the emergency service had been contacted, and Marie was conveyed to hospital where, at 8.15am, she was pronounced dead.

Police officers, who had attended the station car park within minutes of receiving a 999 call, launched a manhunt for Flore who later was arrested by armed police officers as he headed towards Three Bridges Railway Station.

When arrested, Flore denied stabbing his girlfriend, telling police officers, that Stephanie had stabbed herself whilst they were having an argument. He was later charged with her murder.

On 19 February 2025, following a trial at Hove Crown Court, which lasted almost three weeks, Jason Flore was found guilty of the wilful murder of his partner Stephanie Marie and sentenced to life imprisonment with a recommendation that he serve a minimum of twenty-one years.

Attempt to Murder a Special Constable

At about 9.30pm on Saturday, 7 September 2024, a British Transport Police Special Constable was on duty outside Preston Railway Station, ensuring the safety of passengers attending the Radio 2 Summer Festival which was taking place in the city.

The officer was unaware that 54-year-old Russell Smith, of Shakespeare Road, Preston had been following him as he performed his duties. Smith approached the constable and stood a few feet behind him, staring at him whilst holding a kitchen knife which was concealed inside his trousers.

As the officer started to walk into the station, Smith pulled the knife from his trousers, raised it above his head and ran towards the officer, before stabbing him in the back, just below his neck. The force of the blow caused the officer to fall forwards, and as he tried to regain his balance, Smith again lunged towards him with the knife, but the constable was able to fend off his attacker and avoid being repeatedly stabbed.

Another police officer, who was standing nearby, heard the commotion, saw the attack unfolding and ran to assist his colleague. Smith was eventually overpowered by the two officers, dropped the knife and was handcuffed before being arrested. The injured officer was conveyed to hospital. The whole incident was recorded on CCTV installed at Preston station.

Following his arrest and detention, Smith smeared his own faeces over the walls of his cell and shouted out that he would attack more officers. He also asked if the policeman he stabbed was dead. Smith was later charged with attempted murder and being in possession of an offensive weapon.

In February 2025, Russell Smith appeared before Preston Crown Court where he pleaded not guilty to both charges. The jury was shown CCTV footage of the incident. Smith admitted being the person in the footage who stabbed the officer but stated that he could not remember anything about the incident and in any event, he did not consider it was attempted murder because he only stabbed the officer once. He went on to say that he must have found the knife, but he could not explain his actions at all. He further stated that he was suffering from mental health problems and needed help.

On Thursday, 27 February, a jury at Preston Crown Court found Smith guilty of attempted murder and possessing an offensive weapon. The case was adjourned until 14 April for sentencing.

On Monday 14 April 2025. Smith again appeared before Preston Crown Court for sentencing. He was sentenced to twenty-three years imprisonment. The judge stated that Smith must serve a minimum of eighteen years before he can be considered for parole, with an extended five years on licence.

About the Author

MALCOLM CLEGG had a thirty-year career as a constable and sergeant in the British Transport Police. Most of his service was spent both in Uniformed and CID policing of the railways and docks at Newport, Cardiff, Port Talbot, and Swansea. He spent ten years in London, stationed at Paddington, Liverpool Street, Stratford, and on the London Underground Network.

The final ten years of his service were spent as a detective sergeant based in Swansea, investigating crimes committed on the Docks and Railway premises over an extensive area of South and West Wales, which included Fishguard Harbour, incorporating the then Sealink ferry services which operated between Fishguard and Rosslare in Ireland.

After his retirement, he became an active member of the British Transport Police History Group (www.btphg.org.uk). He has carried out extensive research on behalf of the group and has written several articles. He has written five other books: *British Steam Locomotives before Preservation; The Last Days of British Steam; LMS and LNER Steam Locomotives; British Transport Police (A definitive history)*, and *Railway Crimes Committed in Victorian Britain*, each published by Pen & Sword Books.

He lives in Swansea where he has lived for almost fifty years.